Unveiling the mind of God

With

The-I-theory

(The inevitable theory)

AZ Khan

Copyright © 2013 by AZ Khan

All rights reserved.

ISBN: 10: **1470101327**
ISBN-13:**978-1470101329**

To my Mother
&
To the Humanity

CONTENTS

Preface

Introduction : The awakening   1

The origin   12

Who am I?   27

The way to immortality   57

The universe and Time   88

Paradox of freewill   104

Another judgment day   118

Evidence in the Evolution   125

Conclusion: The reasoning   137

Preface

This book represents a compact interpretation of a new scientific theory about the origin of the universe titled "The inevitable theory," or the-I-theory. The-I-theory is a collection of logical conclusions inferred directly from first-person subjective reasoning. This theory is a non-physical scientific theory that literally answers all our ontological fundamental questions including the big question, "why there is something rather than nothing?" The-I-theory perfectly solves all mysteries about human consciousness, which is considered as the most intractable subject in the history of human understanding. The theory not only explains how consciousness arises within organisms in a subjective manner, it also explains its (consciousness) relationship with the objective reality. The theory introduces two new fundamental problems of first-person subjective consciousness that philosophers and scientific minds on this subject have failed to grasp until now. These two newly revealed problems are absolutely vital and unavoidable for any human being living on this planet. These two problems indicate a restriction for any physical theory to have successfully overcome the problems of the origin of the universe; and thus these make the-I-theory inevitable. By solving these two fundamental problems of consciousness, the-I-theory evidently resolves all fallacies of science and religion, and reveals the underlying secrets of the **life-and-death cycle** of conscious humans. Therefore, anyone would realize that this book has become a 'must read' for thoughtful individuals, from any religion, any race and any ideals, who enthusiastically want to know their real identity.

With respect to Creation and God system, the-I-theory does not support any religious or spiritual concept anyway, and very surprisingly, it also does not support traditional atheism. The theory only removes an invisible curtain from our eyes and unveils the mind of a new God—a God who suffers for his or her own deeds, and who can truly bring happiness to humankind!

The fundamental reasoning of this theory, I, actually, acquired in my childhood as a normal human being. It took me long years to find its compatibility with the systems of the physical universe. I thought that my theories would be expressed in their real meanings no better in a thesis paper than as a book. That is why I dare to present it now as a book directly to the general people. The subject matter of this book generally spreads over wide areas of science and philosophy, but I have made the book compact and less detailed with a view to introduce only the basic concepts of the-I-theory to general people primarily. Though the-I-theory can explain any fundamental problem from any realm of science and metaphysics, I have tried to cover some the most important problems here in which lay people would be interested along with professional scientists and philosophers. I would like to expand the implementations of the theory to the other problem areas of science, including quantum reality and gravity, in the expanded version of this book. I have tried my best to make the book simple and accessible to general readers avoiding all unnecessary philosophical and scientific complications. Any kind of critical analysis of this theory from anyone anywhere will be appreciated.

A Z khan
27-05-2013

Introduction: The awakening

Do you know why and how you were born as a human being? Do you know, what is going to happen to you after you die? Do you think, what science and religion told you so far were true? You can discover it yourself now—with the help of the-I-theory.

What is the ultimate purpose of the human's quest of knowledge? Is it to understand our origin, or is it to understand the origin of the universe? Humans, who appeared first on this planet two hundred thousand years ago, asked three questions, nonverbally, from their wonder: who are we, where are we, and where have we come from? Standing in the front-yard of twenty-first century, we are still asking the same questions. In the meantime, we have passed, more or less, twelve thousand years of effective civilization, we have faced countless catastrophes made by nature and by ourselves; unknown amount of water has been passed by the rivers Mississippi, Nile and Volga—we have failed to know our origin. Are we created by a supernatural being called God, or are we originated from 'nobody', in a chance, called quantum fluctuations—we still do not know the answer. However, from the very ancient times, we had been trying to understand the secrets of the existence of the universe by observing the systems of nature. Consequently, we started gazing at the far galaxies. We discovered hundreds of laws of nature in the realm of physics, chemistry and biology. We now consider ourselves to have arrived at the doorway of understanding the whole universal system—but is this really the fact? Are we truly approaching the right path of understanding the fundamental systems of the universe?

Humans always felt insignificant comparing them with the abundance of the heavens. Therefore, they always seek answers of their fundamental questions looking at the courses of the planets and stars. As a result, gathering bit by bit from the ancient times, now we have a rich database of information in the fields of astrophysics and cosmology. However, the development of modern astrophysics and cosmology actually started from the seventeenth century along the way of Giordano Bruno, Tyco Brahe, Johannes Kepler, Nicolas Copernicus and Galileo Galilei. Later theoretical physicists and mathematicians like: Newton, Einstein, Maxwell, Plank, Dirac, Feynman, and with the work of many other dedicated scientists, we think we have ultimately accomplished the mission of our quest of knowledge. Invention of highly effective research satellites like COBE, Hubble space telescope and colossal particle accelerators like the LHC in CERN has given us the farthest sight to the macroscopic and the finest to the microscopic world. We have figured out and formulated the most fundamental four forces of nature. At last, with our great confidence, we have stepped into the hallway of discovering the Final theory that Albert Einstein dreamed of—the theory of unification of physics, and the answer to all questions about the universe.

Our question is, can the theory that supposed to unify physics, answer all questions about the universe? We can hope that our dreams of unification of physics would eventually come to reality someday, but that is not all we want for our ultimate intellectual gratification. If all the problems of physics were solved by now, we would still remain stuck in the same position, as we were at the beginning of understanding, solving just one fundamental problem—the problem of origin! Why the universe is existed and how we are here, are the problems we have failed to explain with any satisfying theory in various attempts within the last several decades. Whether this 'origin' thing seems inexplicable or not, we know, this problem is unavoidable for us. We cannot claim that we understand all systems of the universe without understanding its origin! So, before writing down a final theory—not more than one inch long (!), we must solve this fundamental problem from a real scientific vantage point. We could expect that our observational science would give us a reasonable answer sooner or later someday, but most of us do not know the De facto that there is an Everest standing in the way of our all understanding, which is our own subjective consciousness! We can feel our subjective consciousness physically, but we cannot measure it with some yardstick made by us. We humans are like the sole distributors of subjective consciousness in this planet and, probably, in the whole universe. If I, you, and all other humans were not here then the universe was anybody's big headache. How would we come to know that discovering only the physical systems of the universe could give us the assurance of unveiling the secrets of our own existence? How can we be certain that the creation of any universe can give the guarantee of creating an individual human being with his or her subjective consciousness? Could there any universe be created where you or I could never be created? There is no doubt about it that we are a part of this physical universe, but do we really understand which one is depending on which one here? Between the universe and humanity, which ensures the existence of the other? Are we just a byproduct of this materialistic system? Or, our existence ensures the existence of a physical universe, and vice-versa? We all (including scientists) were born into a ready-made universe and then we started asking about its origin. Who would ask about the origin of the universe if there were no conscious humans here? Ignoring these fundamental questions and the questioners themselves, at times, we believed in scientific determinism. We thought that the initial condition of the universe determines the existence of everything including us. However, the castle of determinism tumbled soon after we were able to gaze at the fundamental levels of matter. We had seen, with our great surprise, that some of the behavior of fundamental particles is beyond the laws we established so far. We came to realize that the reality in quantum level is defined absolutely by us—the observers, and which we do not define, it remains uncertain there! This reality confused us profoundly and we established the "uncertainty" again; but can this uncertainty explain our certain existence?

The clash between quantum phenomenon and classical reality actually began from this point. Quantum and classical world cannot be two different worlds. All classical objects are primarily made of quantum objects. So how can an uncertain world create a certain environment we see in our everyday life— where a stone never changes its position behind our eyes without any reason, and no one can walk through the walls.

The calamity over uncertainty continued in another totally different way. While observing the fundamental laws of the universe, scientists 'accidentally' discovered that the universe is finely tuned. They found that the universe we see is literally balancing on the blade of a sword. Little trembling or variations in parameters will make the whole familiar universe collapsing into an inhospitable shape instantly. The question arose, how there was only one accurate parameter chosen for every fundamental system of the universe where uncertainty reigns in the origin! Still now, this discovery is chasing scientists like

Frankenstein's creature. Some theologians and 'religious intellectuals' immediately snatched this surprising fact in their own favor and they drew teleological arguments out of graves, covering modern suits of "intelligent design", which was considered well refuted by David Hume and Charles Darwin long ago. However, a way of trying to recover from this unpleasant situation some scientists proposed to accept idealistic and rather incomplete explanations of the anthropic principle, and associated Multiverse concept with it, which actually made the water even muddier.

Now we have evidences in cosmological parameters, in quantum phenomena and in the process of biological evolution that our consciousness is playing a crucial role in the universal systems. But what is our definite position here? Are we just passive observers who have nothing to do but facing our own existence? Are we only the helpless victims of the will of an autocratic supernatural God? Or are we just some byproduct of an accidental quantum event? Our first-person subjective consciousness tells us another story; that is, all our subjective experiences like our feeling of pain, sorrows, happiness, hope, our understandings and all which we get through our cognitive process, is absolutely belongs to us. Nobody can give us this self-experience, as a gift or a curse, even if he or she is fulfilling all criteria of a God. We are here in this world giving the testimony of our own individual self-existence, and we cannot share it with anybody or anything in the universe. We always feel this undeniable truth with our senses that each and every human is living individual, who are solely responsible for their own existence.

Renowned physicist Robert Feynman once doubted about our understandings of quantum reality. Whether it is true or not is a matter of argument still now, but no one would disagree that what most of us do not understand properly is our own subjective consciousness. Something has to be worried about that physicists are also included in this category. The question is, why we should care about whether physicists understands subjective consciousness or not. Some might say, the question of origin belongs to philosophy and metaphysics only, and physicists are not responsible to answer these questions. But according to Professor Stephen Hawking, philosophy is no more! Therefore (after returning from the funeral), physicists could not help holding this on their shoulders. The allied forces of theoretical physics, astrophysics, cosmology and mathematics made a rigorous effort in their own way of solving this problem. But, unfortunately, after several unsuccessful attempts with highly mathematical super gravity and super string theory, they are now, literally, praying for the high-bred M theory to survive as the theory of everything. We do not know how the M theory would account for consciousness, and scientists confirmed that whatever the result, it is going to remain only within the experts in the certain fields because of its eleven dimensional mathematical qualities. Therefore, we should not hope that M theory would give us any answer of our fundamental questions in a language understandable to laymen like us in near or far future.

There was a matter of great hope and curiosity for us that, in the meantime, renowned physicist and mathematician Roger Penrose and some others with him considered this 'neglected' matter in a humane way. Somehow, their tremendous mathematical brain calculated a relationship between quantum reality and human consciousness. Penrose understood that a true "theory of everything" must include consciousness. Penrose's statements about consciousness remain as milestones for consciousness in the way of invading the mainstream science. However, for the habit of traditional practice, they were also headed in the wrong way. They seemed only interested in finding the objective quantum mechanism by which consciousness can be emerged in our brain. Anyone can realize that there must be a quantum mechanism and a neurological mechanism remain for consciousness to arise, but these cannot be the last words for subjective consciousness. The problem of consciousness is only with its subjective part; Roger Penrose and his colleagues were yet to be realized this fact. Many philosophers, who have tried to explain consciousness from just an objective viewpoint, have recently shown some other fascinating but hopeless efforts. American philosopher Daniel Dennett is one of the most influential amongst them. He stated that individual humans are not the authority on their own subjective experience as they think they are, and consciousness can be explained using a third person method from the outside. However, those who thinks consciousness can be explained from an objective viewpoint only, and it is just a hard problem, the-I-theory can make consciousness harder for them. Sarcastically, one the purposes of this book is to show the hardest part of subjective consciousness, before solving it, which cognitive scientists and neurologists had never imagined.

We can never imagine that there are so many fundamental problems remain which are directly related with the problem of consciousness. We still do not know how our free will becomes compatible with physical laws of nature. We still do not know a proper definition of what we call 'time'. We do not know why quantum objects behave such weirdly; we cannot imagine how a boundary of the universe may look like. In addition, from other aspects, we do not know why there is only one intelligent species remains on earth amongst millions. We don't even know how can we prove or disprove a God theory scientifically; so how can we be so confident that we can give all answers with a physical theory, which would be not more than one inch long, and which can be testified empirically? Along with the satisfaction of all our achievements, we are still asking questions, "Have God had any choice creating the universe?", or, "Why there is something rather than nothing?" These are not just simple questions of general people; nowadays, experts are asking these, and it seems they are also seeking answers through common sense.

However, at this stage of development in science and technology, we must have the ability to overcome our ignorance about these fundamental problems. From cosmological and metaphysical standpoint, one question should be straightforward, can we understand the fundamental system of our existence or not? Is it possible to understand why and how there is a universe exists including us, either with the help of our common sense, or with complex mathematical formulations beyond our general knowledge?

The-I-theory (the inevitable theory), described in this book, gives an affirmative and clear-cut answer of this question. The-I-theory is not a "grand unified theory" of forces or not a "theory of everything" of traditional fashion. It stands inevitably before all physical theories as it can explain the fundamental reason of the existence of the universe that physical theories have failed to explain. The-I-theory takes a fatal slash upon the fallacies of any divine design concept and accidental quantum fluctuation theory, by bringing both under the fundamental scientific jurisdiction, which were crying to explain the origin of the universe for centuries. Ultimately, the-I-theory comes up with an extraordinary conclusion by establishing Humanity, with its supremacy and magnificence, up above anything in this universe.

The-I-theory unveils the grand reason, or the cause for the rise of human consciousness along with the universe. It solves all fundamental problems of almost every branch of science. With the proper implementation of the- I-theory, scientists can get rid of this burden of explaining the apparent inexplicable. The-I-theory reveals the underlying secrets—what is actually going on here in this universe. It reveals our real identity: who we are, what we are, what we are doing here, how we come to life as an individual human being and what happens after our death. We shall be surprised to know the truth beyond the truth about the universe and about us. We can assure you, this story will be a far different story than which we ever heard, and this is going to hurt all of our scientific, philosophical and religious prejudices severely.

The origin
(Solving the fundamental problem)

Almost in all religious textbooks and creation-mythologies described the origin of the universe in a non-radical—customary manner. There was always a starting point in chaos or in nothingness. The reason of creation stated in the same way almost in all religions— at first there was only God exists, he was alone and, somewhat, bored. There was nobody to worship him. So he created the universe, subsequently, celestial bodies, earth, plants, animals and, at last humans. Some races of humans denied to worship him, or disobeyed his laws, so he destroyed them and created another race, and so on.

For many of us, these descriptions seem enough for the explanation of the origin of the universe, but others, who cannot enthusiastically keep faith in these fairy tales, would go one-step backward finding the explanation about the total existence—including God. We could expect that modern observational cosmology would give us a better solution at this point, but these observations and associated hypotheses are also limited only to the first point of creation, not beyond that.

Astrophysicists and cosmologists were so much intrigued by the condition of the universe, in the first three minutes or in the first hundred billionth of a second, after the Big bang. However, laymen do not always use to see everything in a 'scientific' way. They were much more fascinated about the three minutes, or a zillionth of a second, before the Big bang. Obviously, both religious myths and traditional science proved undeserving for this fascination of curious people. Theologians sometimes stated God as a self-originated being; that means, God has been created by itself from nothingness. This solution clearly doesn't break the uprightness of a usual childish question—why can't other things be created by itself like God? So we urge to the physics and cosmology for the answer because we know that, in the new world, physicists and cosmologists are the self-claimed dominating power in this realm. But the best they could tell us about this problem within the last several decades, to keep our mouth shut: "there is nothing north of north pole" (Stephen Hawking), and "nothing is actually something" (Lawrence M. Krauss)—this is frustrating.

Why we ask such questions like—why there is something rather than nothing? We see clear emphasis in this question on 'nothing' than 'something'. It is because we think nothingness is perfect. There is nothing wrong with the thinking that if there is no energy, no matter, no 'nothing' remain, then there only remains perfect calmness of nothingness. So, why there any energy should fluctuate, without any reason, to disrupt this perfect calmness? If we think, there is a primordial energy state always remains and this energy naturally occurs random fluctuations, here and there, like a problem child, then it seems it is ok. But when we think these random fluctuations accidentally caught the perfect four forces to build this cosmos, and perfectly regulated biological evolution to create humans like us, (who are somewhat annoyed with this 'unauthorized' performance of energies) then this is nothing but the brilliance of our deceived imagination. It is undeniable that if the universe could come out of nothing creating a meaningful shape without any cause, then anything could come out of nothing at any time without any cause. If this could really happen in reality then there was nothing weird to expect that things like the Eiffel tower and the Statue of Liberty coming out of nowhere, at any time in any place.

How could we know the answer—did the universe come out of a chance, or had it a predominant cause that it must come out like this? If the chance theory is true, then there is a big contradiction comes within, we could never know the reason of origin using any laws of science because there is no reason at all! So, why we are trying so hard to understand this reason of origin with the scientific laws? Contrarily, if there was no chance or no accidental event happened here, then we must have a clue—the existence of the universe was certain (as it is existed now). There was a certainty that the universe must come into existence, so there must be an unavoidable condition, in the first place, acted as a certain reason for the 'rise' of the universe.

Think about an imaginary situation. Suppose you are left in a closed room blindfolded and when you release yourself from blindfold, you come to know that the room is pitch-black. If you are previously informed that there has a trapdoor in the room then you will try to find the door immediately, and you could come out quickly and easily. But if you do not have any instructions what to do or how to come out, you will primarily fall in a confusion. However, as you are a human being, and you have your natural eagerness to come out of that unpleasant situation, you won't just stay there—doing nothing. You, certainly, would try to find out if there is a trapdoor in the room or not. You will start checking every wall inch by inch, and finding out of the door is just a matter of time only. Even if you are not previously informed, when there is a certainty that there is a trapdoor to come out, when the room space is finite, and when you want to be freed from that situation, your possibility of finding the door is hundred percent.

But in the case of universal existence (total existence) the situation was quite different. If the universe had no unavoidable bindings for emerging, then it wouldn't go for it anyway; therefore, no energy would induce the universe, from something or from nothing, in search of a state called existed, and it will remain 'blindfolded' forever. So what could be the certain reason or 'inevitable condition' for the emerging of the universe? How could we find it inferring logically from fundamental premises? Before we go for it, let us try to find a clue from the famous fundamental question about the origin, which we consider unsolved to humankind.

"Why there is something rather than nothing?" This is the greatest ontological question about the origin. Some like to ask this in a different way. "Why there is a universe exists instead of nothingness?" We usually believe that, these two questions are originally the same question where the word 'something' is equivalent to the existence of the universe and nothing means nonexistence of the universe. So, If we neglect the 'universe' for a while, we shall see that this is actually a question of existence and nonexistence only. If we write down the question, such a way so that it perfectly reflects the meanings from our thoughts, then that would be, "why there is existence rather than nonexistence?", but is this a valid question? Our point is, nonexistence is indefinable, and therefore, it cannot be a valid subject matter in arguments with existence. If existence is only definable between existence and nonexistence, then another question definitely comes prior to this—what is an existence, or how can we label something as existence? What are philosophers used to say about existence that would be a little 'frightening' for some of us; let us try if we could find any fundamental property of existence using our common sense only.

In the real world, anything, which we observe, realize or experience with our senses, is considered existed. The question is why we need to observe, realize or experience something to mark it as existence, or what is the primary purpose of this process? Certainly, this observing process, involving our sensory organs, helps us to recognize or detect something as an existence. So the primary purpose of the process is only recognizing, or to compare it with an 'existence' previously known. If any existence is not recognizable then we cannot claim it as an existence. This is a restriction or unavoidable condition for any candidate of existence.

On the other hand, a recognizing agent is necessary for any recognizing process. Generally, we use ourselves, reliable third parties, or established laws of science in any recognizing process of existence. All three of them, or any two can be involved in a recognizing process; but a single agent is absolutely necessary for recognizing an existence. This is another restriction.

Let us see, in the real world, how something becomes an existence. We shall take a human being, a golf ball and a Muon particle as candidates for existence.

A human being can be recognized by its own. A third person or another human being can recognize that human being as an existence. We do not need any scientific formulation to prove the existence of a human being. So we can say that the particular human being is an existence.

A golf ball cannot recognize itself as an existence. But a human being, as a third party, can recognize it easily. So the golf ball is also an existence. Same way, a Muon particle cannot recognize itself as an existence. A human being cannot also recognize it as an existence physically. But the laws of science can recognize it by observing its effect in a particle accelerator. So the Muon particle is an existence.

Now take a Unicorn and Higg's Boson particle as candidates of existence. Mythical character Unicorn cannot recognize itself (as it is supposed to be an animal). A third party or a human being never recognized it as an existence. So unicorn is not an existence, it is nonexistence. Higgs Boson is the basic element of the standard model of particles. The Higgs boson has recently been detected or recognized in particle accelerators (?) So it is now an existence, and it was surely nonexistence before it was detected. There are also many things, which have disputes about their existence. For instance, some say, they have identified the Unidentified Flying Objects or UFOs. Others do not approve this; they say that it (UFO) has not been witnessed by a reliable recognizing process. So the argument is whether the recognizing process is reliable or not, there is no argument about whether it has to be recognized or not.

From this brief discussion, we can conclude that a recognizing process and a recognizing agent are absolutely necessary to prove something as an existence. In the absence of a recognizing agent, or If the recognizing process fails, the candidate of existence must be considered as nonexistence. This conclusion leads us to formulate the principle of existence as follows:

"Without any exception, to be an existence, anything has to be recognized by a recognizing agent as an existence."

In other words, anything must be recognizable to an agent to become existence.

Now the question of existence or nonexistence of the universe comes within. Our question was, "Why there is existence rather than nonexistence?" The way to solve this question first we have to define the nature or properties of existence and nonexistence that we are talking about in this specific question. Notice that by the word existence or nonexistence it does not mean the existence or nonexistence of a human being or a golf ball or a Muon particle etc. It definitely means the existence or nonexistence of the universe as a whole. Where there is a question of existence or nonexistence as a whole, nothing can remain outside of existence, and the same way, nothing can remain inside of nonexistence. We shall take the term universal existence for existence and universal nonexistence for nonexistence to value it as a whole. So we get the properties as follows:
1. There cannot be anything remained outside of the universal existence.
2. There must be something remained within the universal existence.

So, universal existence must have something within it.

Again,

1. There cannot be anything remained outside of the universal nonexistence.
2. There cannot be anything remained within the universal nonexistence.

So, universal nonexistence must have nothing within or outside of it.

As we can see, the first property is same for both universal existence and universal nonexistence.

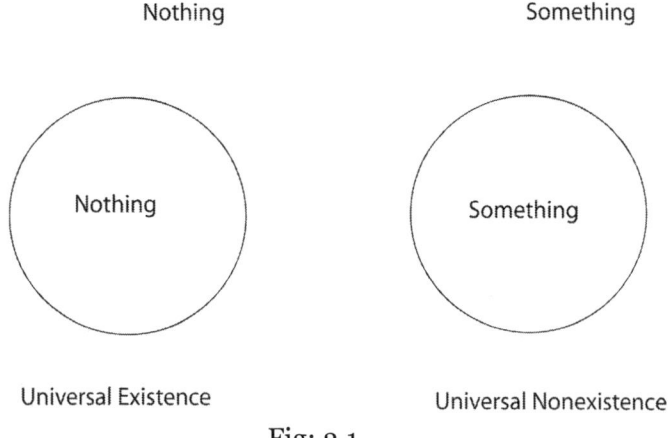

Fig: 2.1

The second property varies between each other. So If we exchange the second property with each other, we should expect to see that universal existence and universal nonexistence immediately changes their identity and replaces to one another. But, as a matter of fact, this doesn't happen so easily with respect to the universe.

If that 'something' does not approve the universal existence by recognizing, then there is no difference remains between universal existence and universal nonexistence. So, universal existence also remains as universal nonexistence when it is not recognized by an agent! This is how recognizing or detecting remains inevitable for both existence and nonexistence.

Let us start again from the beginning to understand this thoroughly. Why there is something rather than nothing? This question is actually a tricky question because there is a contradiction remains within the question itself, and the answer lies in this contradiction. Assume that there is only nothingness exists. Then our question would be, "why there has nothingness existed?" But how can we ask this question if we are not there? If we could imagine a picture of that state, we would see that everything (the laws of physics—to be more scientific) breaks down into total nothingness, nothing can induce from there, not even a single fluctuation, and it remains unchangeable forever. Though, we have an intuition that nothing is like a 'thing' that is detectable. We usually use sentences like "there is nothing in the box", where we know that it is detectable that there is nothing in the box. But this example cannot be analogous with total nothingness. Where there is only nothingness exists, then no one or nothing remains there to detect that state—that is why it is the nonexistence state. So nothingness always remains unquestioned. We cannot ever ask—why there is nothing—by going into the total nothingness. Now hypothetically consider that there is something exists as the universe. So, how could we know that there is really something exists? We are going to get the same answer—we know there is something because we can recognize it—there cannot be another answer to this question. But when no one recognizes it as something, then who gets and transfers the information about that something? So there will be no difference remains, between nothing and that hypothetical something, when it is not recognized or detected. The condition is same in both cases, nothing and something, a recognizing agent is absolutely necessary to approve their existence. As we marked earlier, our usual belief is, nothing is nonexistence and something is existence. But, the fact is, when it is recognized universally by a recognizing agent, we'll never get total nothingness, we'd always get something as the universe. So when recognizing is inevitable for both nothing and something, total nonexistence is impossible, and total existence is absolute. The universe can never go to nonexistence because there is nothing called nonexistence as a whole. That is why we see a universe, not nothingness, and that is why there is something rather than nothing, period.

Whatever it is, something or nothing, cannot remain unrecognized—this is the inevitable condition of universal existence. The-I-theory implies this inevitable condition as the grand reason of the origin of the universe.

Now we can easily infer the principle of Universal existence from this stipulation.

"Universal existence is bound to remain existed as it has no opposite phase."

In other words, the universe will remain existed forever recognized by a recognizing agent, as it (the universe) has no other choice.

Now we shall find out the initial mechanism of the emerging of the universe. When this inevitable condition (recognizing) acts predominantly, universal existence cannot stay at rest for a moment. Therefore, the inevitable condition induces the universal potential energy into an active energy. The energy of universal existence (EUX), as we have termed it here, then splits into matter and energies to conduct a restless effort to fulfill the condition. As a result, catching the perfect laws and systems, the universe is created and, ultimately, recognized as an existence. We can assume that the energy of universal existence would try to sustain this position inevitably, forever along eternity, or creating and destroying the universal system perpetually, as it has no other choice.

Why we see a universe like this? Why we see a universe systematic and guided by laws? Why it is not just chaotic? Now we know that there is a cause behind it that it can catch any laws only to be recognized.

Now what about the recognition process? Is it independent of universal existence? The properties of universal existence say that there cannot be anything beyond universal existence. So the recognition process must occur within the universal existence; it can be the whole universal system or a part of it. So in the case of the universe, the recognition process must be created within the universe and by the universe itself. So we can say, the universe is being recognized by itself. There is no third party here, independent of the universe, what is involved in this recognition process.

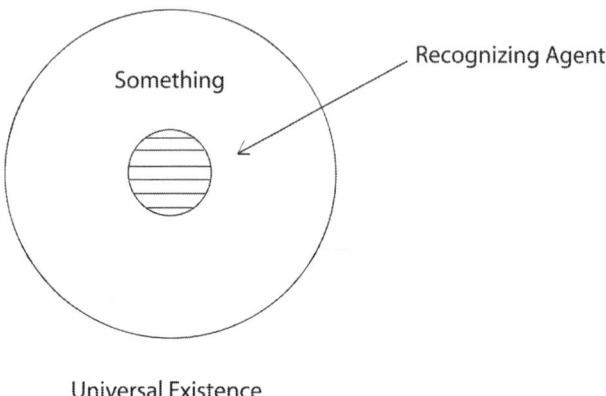

Fig: 2.2

So we can write down the principle of universal self-existence or **the subjective universal principle** as follows:

The Universe is absolute as an existence, and it will remain existed forever recognized by its own, as it has no other choice.

Now we get, the universal existence is absolute. So in the case of absolute universe, certainly, it is being recognized by a certain recognition process and by a certain recognizing agent in order to fulfill the condition. And when the universe is the total existence (there is nothing outside of it), then it must have been self-recognized. **When self-recognizing is compulsory, subjectivity is inevitable for the universe**. So there must have something physically exists within the universe by which the universe is feeling itself subjectively and fulfilling the condition of self-recognition. Which do you think has the best subjective parts of the universe that supposed to fulfill the condition of self-recognizing for the universe except humans—the stars, Galaxies, Black holes, Quasars, Pulsars, Dark matters, Red woods, Mastodons, T-Rex, Grasshoppers, Allegis, Bucky balls, Photons?

Now we have got a complete picture in our mind. The first fluctuations did not occur without reasons—quantum fluctuations in nothingness were unavoidable for the universe. The universe emerged catching definite laws only to be self-recognized—to fulfill the definition of existence only. At the primordial state, the whole process of the universal system was targeted to create a self-recognition process and a self-recognizing agent. Material systems were not enough for these targeted achievements, so, complex biological systems involved. Humans just have fallen as victims for this definition of existence—as they have become the final product. This is the mechanism of the origin and existence of the universe. This mechanism is simple as it appears; there is no 'mathematically tractable' or supernatural cause remains behind this. Individual humans always came out of nowhere and fell in the hazards of direct experience. Persuaded by their encoded instincts they struggled against the violence of nature only to remain existed. Sometimes they felt themselves vulnerable comparing to the destructive power of nature, so sometimes they tried to make their 'insignificant' existence meaningful by remaining indulged in their own made spirituality.

Why should we believe in this solution for the origin of the universe? Is this just another postulation, which we could never prove empirically? The answer is no; there is at least one possible way to prove it empirically, but the way is obstructed by an apparent intractable puzzle—the puzzle of consciousness. Henceforth, from the next chapter, we are going to walk through the most clogged areas of science and philosophy—solving the puzzle of consciousness.

Who am I?
(The 'hardest' problem of consciousness)

I had a problem. I had been carrying this problem for many years from my childhood. Let's see if you had the same problem like me or not. My problem had been just with myself. In fact, I was my problem.

When I was just six or seven years old, I perceived a strange feeling of myself that, I was not supposed to be existed! I could not clearly express that feeling to myself, at that time, but it gave me some vague understandings like this: I know I am here in this world, I know I have my parents and siblings, but I don't know why or how, or from where I am here in this world. But I am just here! How am I here? What am I doing here? These questions were not just thoughts in words to me at all. These were some unique feelings of individuality and loneliness, which I used to get at that time.

The moment a human being gets conscious, his or her reality starts from that very moment. When a human child is born, his (means no gender) consciousness is also born with him. At that primary stage, his brain remains quite immature, so his consciousness also remains limited. At that time, only the child's instincts kept him alive. His hunger and thirst tell him when he needs for feeding, and his sense of smell tells him where to look around. As time goes by, slowly, the child's brain gets enough mature that nothing in the world can escape from his awareness; and at the same time, he gets another feeling that strangely separates away his body and mind from anything in the world—he becomes self-conscious. Obviously, the problem I had in my childhood was with my self-consciousness or subjective consciousness or first-person consciousness only.

Now, what are these consciousness and self-consciousness we are talking about and why are we talking about this, in the way of explaining the origin, anyway? Every human being knows what consciousness and self-consciousness is; he or she can feel it every moment in his or her life whenever they concentrate on anything in the world and whenever they concentrate on themselves avoiding everything in the world. There is nothing so intimately we can observe or feel in the world than the feeling of our consciousness and self-consciousness. Practically, the world comes alive to us after we get consciousness and the world instantly disappears from us when we lose consciousness. Only sentient beings like humans and animals act like agents to experience subjective perception of the outside world through consciousness and self-consciousness. We are talking about this not because these are now the hot topics in the scientific and philosophical community; we need to talk about this because there is something wrong with this. Yes, there is something seriously and 'scientifically' wrong with our consciousness and self-consciousness. There is an obvious anomaly dwells behind our eyes with consciousness and self-consciousness, which can turn the direction of our quest of the ultimate knowledge instantly. This problem is very much physical, fundamental, and closer to humans than anything else, but for a very strange and unknown reason, our scientists and philosophers (who are also humans) has failed to recognize it until now.

We usually think consciousness is a term mostly refers to philosophy, psychology and Neuroscience. However, for more than two thousand years, human conscious and self-consciousness also remains a mystery to scientists of all groups, theologians and to the general people. From the very primal times of civilization, many thinkers and philosophers have been expressing their own ideas about consciousness in spiritual, idealistic or materialistic way. Religion sometimes has drawn a veil upon our self and subjectivity diverting our concentration to some imaginary Gods or Goddesses. Materialistic doctrines sometime confused us profoundly; scientists' emphasis on empirical exploration converted our direction towards objectivity almost successfully; but the truth is, the mystery of consciousness continues. A proper definition of consciousness still seems unachievable though there have been a flourishing history of consciousness studies of over four centuries. Inspired by the teachings of Buddha and by the work of Roman thinker Cicero, seventeen-century French philosopher René Descartes introduced a concept of consciousness called 'Cartesian dualism,' assuming that consciousness is independent of the materialistic world and the source of consciousness is located in the *pineal gland* in the brain. Later British philosopher John Lock is believed to be established the modern concept of consciousness. He defined consciousness as "the perception of what passes through one's own mind". He also defines the 'self' as " the conscious thinking thing" or as an entity in his *theory of mind*. German philosopher Immanuel Kant was one of the first thinkers to propose the thought that our cognitive experience is independent of materialistic reality, and rather it may be true in the other way. There are numerous scholarly works published, and researches performed in the field of philosophy, psychology and Neuroscience, in modern days, to find out the nature of consciousness; and concluded it as, seemingly, the most inexplicable subject humans dealt so far.

The most difficulty all theorists used to face, while defining consciousness, is that it is absolutely a self-confined experience. It shows an unfavorable characteristic, which seems to resist transferring its raw information identical to another human being. Everyone can experience this from a separate point of view, but it is impossible to experience with everyone at the same time same way from a collective point of view. Therefore, to general people the concept of consciousness always remains a vague idea, and they often fall in confusions when they try to find something analogous with consciousness. There is another quality so notorious regarding consciousness that it seems it gets more complicated when we try to make it simpler by examples. That is why some theorists have come to a frustrating conclusion defining consciousness as only illusive and intractable. Nowadays, consciousness is truly a hot topic all over the world, and it is spreading its obscurity over the minds of the people of almost every branch of science. Renowned physicist and cosmologist Steven Weinberg showed his deep concern in his writings about the problem of consciousness and indicated that this must be the greatest obstacle before a physical theory to overcome successfully the puzzle of the origin of the universe.

Why consciousness appears to be the most stubborn? We know, our all understandings come through consciousness, so, why we cannot understand the system of our own understanding process. It is obvious that consciousness comes from a neurobiological process of our brain: but how can just a neurobiological process give a nonliving object its subjectivity—a self-feeling of existence? Recently, a group of eight neuroscientists confessed their limitations about leashing consciousness in definition stating that it is too early to write down a theory, which is likely to give an effective definition of consciousness. Some readily assert that current physical state of the human brain is unable to define something like consciousness. Some define consciousness is just an illusion of the brain; it has no real aspect at all.

We can assume that, something may be favorable for those scientists who confessed about our limitations of defining consciousness. We can also let alone those "holy men" or spiritual Gurus, who claim that they have become 'enlightened' by unifying themselves with universal consciousness. However, when some scientists claim that, objectively, consciousness can come out from quantum fluctuations in a certain situation without any reason, we cannot help doubting their over fascinations with objective physical reality. If consciousness is a term that refers to first-person only, and when it can give the self-feeling of things then it is anything but an objective occurrence. Consciousness cannot come out from anything, anywhere and anytime making the 'thing' saying, "wow! I am conscious." There might be a certain criterion or threshold exists for the thing, the place, and the time for appearing consciousness, and this threshold might have been maintained by the universal existence fundamentally. As a matter of fact, from an objective point of view, we are not even authorized for giving an explanation on first-person subjective experience, no matter how 'enlightened' we think we are. We should not also consider any third-person assertion of anyone as empirical evidence while defining first-person consciousness. Therefore, everyone, including scientists, must rely on their own first-person experience for analyzing and making a conclusion on first-person consciousness.

In spite of these underlying difficulties, philosophers identified several specific problems of consciousness as the hard problems and some other as the easy problems of consciousness. One of these is the well-known problem called *qualia,* widely popularized by philosopher David J. Chalmers, which is about some qualitative aspects of our mental state, like the raw sensation of pain and pleasure, experience of color like red or green and tastes like sweet or sour. These qualities do not exist physically at all. In the case of color, only different wavelengths of light or electromagnetic radiation exist. Pain, pleasure, taste of sweet and sour comes from different outside stimuli through sensory nerves and through different neurobiological process in our brain. How theses physical processes in our brain create and distinguish these rich meaningful sensations and give us experiences like red, green, blue, pain, pleasure, sweetness, sour is considered as a hard problem of subjective consciousness, well-discussed but remains unsolved so far.

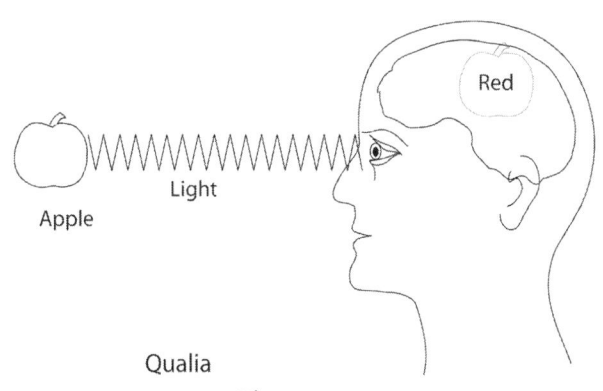

Fig: 3.1

Another problem is called *binding problem*. How our brain processes and accumulate different visual perceptions like color, shape, motion in a single frame and gives us conscious experience of the total picture, where different perceptions may be processed by different and physically separated neurobiological functions, is considered an easy problem of consciousness.

Whether the problems are easy or hard, these problems are not actually the fundamental problems of consciousness. We shall later see that all problems indicated by various theorists originally remain submerged in just one basic problem (specified in this chapter), and solving this fundamental problem solves every other problem of consciousness, easy or hard, perfectly and automatically. Factually, we do not know what really consciousness is, and what is its relation to the universal laws, and, at least, we do not know why the physical universe needs such 'thing' like consciousness—that is why we feel these (qualia or binding problem) as problems.

How can we know, convincingly, with a proper theory, what really consciousness is, or why the physical world need it? If we want to know its relation with the physical world then we need a physical theory, and a physical theory can be acquired only by solving a physical problem. But how can we find a physical problem of consciousness, and how can it be solved with a physical theory when we think consciousness has no physical aspect at all? We must keep in mind that every physical law can be examined empirically, and every force can be transferred from one state to another, where we cannot transfer our conscious experience to anywhere or to anything for experiments.

One might simply wonder is there any mystery about consciousness that lies beyond the physical universe. Is consciousness really elusive, or is it something transcendental? Nevertheless, these assumptions are certainly not true regarding something we call our first-person, because first-person is the place where we have missed the most important problem of consciousness, which is not at all elusive.

Consciousness is physical in just one aspect that is the first-person aspect. First-person is the authority of our subjective individual perception. Each and every physical experience has to be approved by our first-person primarily. In fact, there is nothing so physical we can think than our first-person, but what is the physical problem here that philosophers still do not have a clue about it? People who claim that they have solved consciousness do not even know that their all claims can be doomed with just one question, and it is going to be the hardest question ever faced by humanity. However, many of them indeed came closer to reality intuitively—the reality we want to reveal here in this chapter.

Many theorists try to distinguish consciousness and self-consciousness as objective and subjective experience respectively. We shall see later that there is no difference remains between conscious and self-conscious experiences except in direction of perspectives, and both come from single subjective platform. There is no objective experience exists on either with consciousness or with self-consciousness, both are one subjective phenomenon appears objectively and subjectively at the same time with the same being.

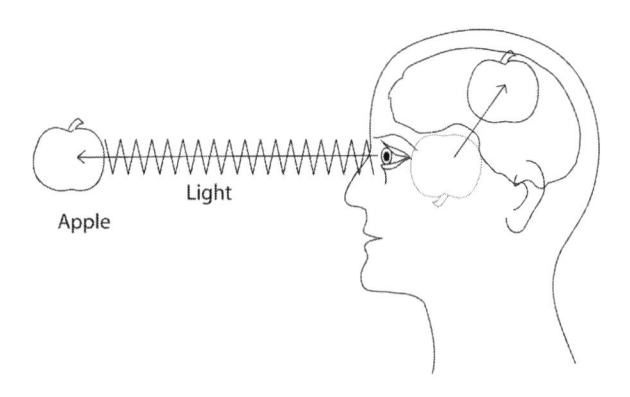

Light
Apple

Subjective Experience of objects

Fig: 3.2

This means when a being is conscious of the outer world, it must be capable of having self-consciousness or first-person consciousness at the same time. Consciousness and self-consciousness both are absolutely dependent on each other, we cannot expect consciousness in total absence of self-consciousness and we cannot expect self-consciousness in total absence of consciousness. Therefore, if we withdraw this discrimination between consciousness and self-consciousness, it will help us a lot understanding their inner properties. However, at first, we need something to be isolated from both consciousness and self-consciousness.

We can simply understand that consciousness is a distinct result of a process, and it is nonphysical when it arises (from objective viewpoint). But what about self-consciousness (from subjective viewpoint)? Self-consciousness is also a nonphysical process, which arises with consciousness and, at the same time, it can feel and approve the process physically. When both processes come from the same origin, reasonably, we can think, both processes must have a common physical origin. We shall take one subjective term 'first-person' as a physical platform for the origin of both consciousness and self-consciousness. This physical platform can be our whole physical body, or only the brain, or it can be just an undefined quantum theater dwells in the brain. For total simplicity, another thing we want to distinguish with consciousness is what we call awareness. Though *awareness* is also an ambiguous term. People usually define awareness analogous with subjective consciousness. However, we shall intentionally specify fundamental differences between awareness and consciousness by defining awareness as the prior state of consciousness only, or the pre-conscious state. At this viewpoint, not everything that is aware is always conscious. A newborn human baby is aware of the outside world but not truly conscious. Plants, most of the animals are aware, and can respond to the stimuli of the outside world with their instincts, but they are not conscious like us. In this notion, we can say that everything including a quantum particle to computer is somewhat aware of something limited, but not conscious as we are. We humans are not also conscious of everything at every moment. For example, our eyes can be pointed to a wall, and at the same time, we may be thinking of something else. In this case, we should not consider that we are conscious of the wall, though we are surely aware of the wall (at least in our definition of awareness). When we fall asleep, we cannot remain conscious of the outside world; neurotransmitters like melatonin, dopamine, create isolation of our sensory nerves from the brain, and then our consciousness only wanders in our memories creating dreams. Therefore, we can say, consciousness comes from our aware concentration, or focus of first-person, to a specific system (physical like objects or nonphysical like thoughts). When this concentration of first-person performs an understanding process successfully regarding the targeted system, then we can call this processing state as the conscious state of our mind. So we can say, Consciousness is an understanding process targeted to a specific system, which comes with the awareness of a physical body along the concentrated focus of first-person.

So we see that there are three individual systems involved within a single process of consciousness. At first, it comes with the awareness of a physical body. Awareness gives rise of the first-person, when first-person concentrates on a system (objective or subjective) and performs the process of understanding of the system then we can say that we are conscious of the system. When first-person concentrates on any system of the outer world, we get our objective understanding, which is "consciousness" in the traditional sense. When first-person concentrates to the origin of first-person, we get our subjective understanding or self-consciousness. So first-person is the common platform for both subjective and objective consciousness. There is one thing so important about consciousness that we cannot be conscious of more than one different system at the same time. It is because we can only focus our mind to a single system at a time to understand it. However, we can swiftly switch our focus to another system, and thus we feel that we are conscious of multiple systems at the same time.

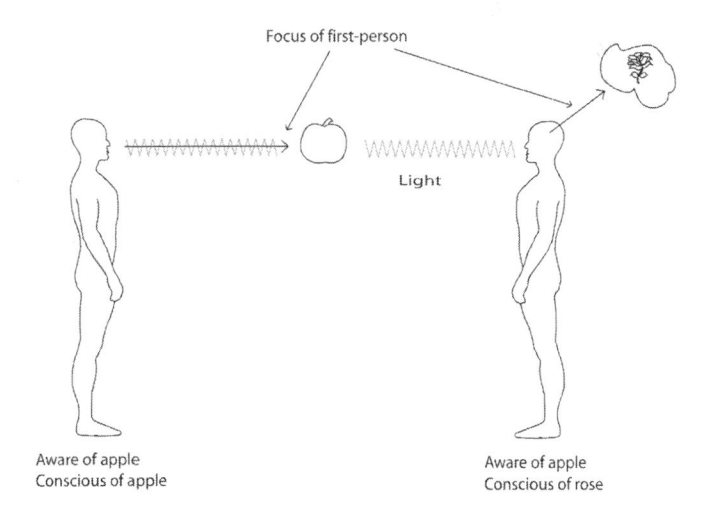

Fig: 3.3

Traditionally, our usual concern is about consciousness or about this process of understanding only. However, it is obvious that if there is nothing acts like first-person, which understands with consciousness primarily, and feel the pain (qualia), then all our understanding or awareness would go futile. If there is nothing says, "I feel that I understand" then how and who is informed whether there any understanding process happened or not. We may be able to make a computer understand many complex systems but if the machine does not say independently, "I feel that I understand" then we must not say that the machine is conscious like us. So things like *qualia* is compulsory for consciousness, and qualia belongs to something which we call our first-person.

So we get, awareness is the state, which makes a sentient being ready for consciousness. When first-person concentrates to a system and gets the understanding, the living body gets proper consciousness. Therefore, proper consciousness is a mutual experience of understanding, involving awareness and associated focus of first person. First-person is the 'thing', which focuses on systems and at the same time acts physically as a subject of understanding. In other words, which physically understands the system is our first-person. The three aspects of consciousness: feeling, concentration and understanding—all are regulated by first-person. However, first-person acts like a subjective platform, not a preexisting thing that always dwells in our brain. When only we get aware and get consciousness then first-person gets vivid to us instead it remains in the dark.

Now, who is the authority of this platform "first-person" that feels, concentrates and understands everything? Is this only belongs to the specific materialistic human body that feels itself as 'I', or is there an unknown entity dwells in our body which feels everything using this materialistic body, or is there any other fundamental system remains that we do not know? The answer is quite surprising with the-I-theory, which we are going to explain here.

Awareness, first-person and understanding of a system—all comes collectively as a single state of experience to human beings, but only for filtering out first-person among them, we have made this classification here. We needed this filtering process because the problem we would like to explain here is not related to our awareness or understanding at all, it is about our first-person only.

First-person gives us the self-feeling—the feeling of our subjectivity. As long as we are conscious, we feel our first-person flawlessly. It seems that every first-person resides in the memory of every individual human being as an individual person. But first-person comes before any personality is created in a human body or before any memory develops. A newborn baby feels pain with its first breath when it is not truly conscious . When the body gets live with awareness it feels its first person right away. We may think that our feeling of first-person is purely nonphysical (as qualia does not have any physical base), but our memory surely has its physical origin. Memory is the reflection of continuous actions of the outside world, acquired through sensory organs, and stored in our brain in some orderly arrangements. Different proteins remain arranged in different unknown forms in our brain and create the base of memory set. We know that our brain is made of hundred billion biological cells called neurons. We also know that continuous electric impulse stimulates (brain waves) neurons and give us the feeling of memory (experience) as well as consciousness (understanding). So first-person arises from a neurobiological base. The human body is made of the known elements like oxygen, carbon, hydrogen, nitrogen, calcium, and phosphorus. All those elements consist of the same kind of atoms and quantum objects that made the materialistic world—the universe. In the previous chapter, we logically established that the universe must have its subjectivity as an inevitable condition. So, as an argument, what you really feel as pain (qualia) cannot be fundamentally belong to you or your specific first-person. The whole universal system—the universe—feels the pain through your first-person and through you—no other 'you' exits independent of this materialistic world. So when you say 'me' to a materialistic body, others say 'me' to the same kind of materialistic body of the same universe. Do not confuse it with your individual personality. Yes, there are some differences in genetic formations, there are differences in experiences in memories, but there is no difference with their materialistic origin. What you feel as 'you' is just the materialistic body which has the-perfect mechanism (neurobiological and quantum) to create the feeling of your first-person, and feels the pain. Therefore, basically, there should not be any fundamental differences remain within those bodies living with you in this world as all bodies have come from the same origin. This is very much easier to understand with a figure:

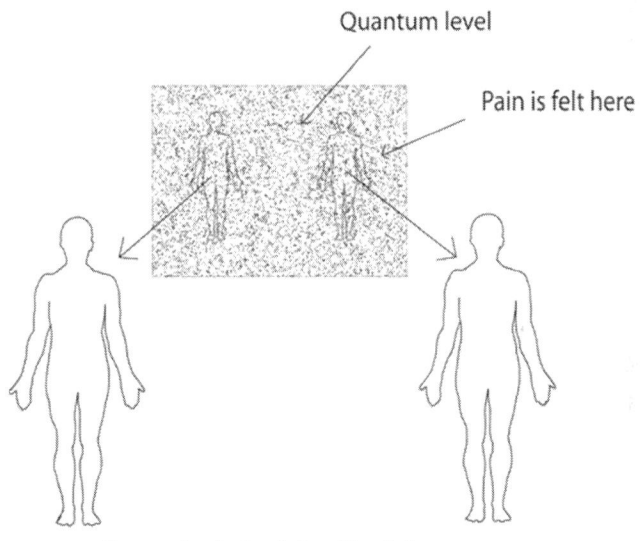

Quantum level

Pain is felt here

Same physical origin of both humans

Fig: 3.4

So what is the problem with this? What is the problem of everyone that they have come from the same materialistic origin? As we have mentioned earlier, there are two distinct problems for living things, especially humans, who have come from the same origin and living together in this world. This problem is with every one of us, separately and individually, but we shall take only 'you' (who is reading this book right now) or your first-person for analytical consideration in this discussion. Reader must keep in mind that these two problems can be realized from first-person subjective viewpoint only. The first problem is about the restriction of transferring information amongst first-persons, which is: **From your subjective point of view, why cannot you feel other living human bodies subjectively?** Another way:

Which mechanism resists transferring subjective information (qualia like pain) identically from one first-person to another—when subjectivity fundamentally belongs to the universe.

As a simpler form, we can say, when the whole universe is governed by the same laws of physics, then any subjective part within the universe supposed to be identical with another subjective part of the same universe. So there should be just one subjective viewpoint (perspective of direct experience) in the universe. But we see separate viewpoints for all individual first-persons—why or how is that so?

The second problem is about the determination of confinement of first-person. There are two distinct parts of this problem. First one is the confinement of first-person within the present living humans, which is:

From your first-person point of view, how do you think it is determined, which one would be you among all living humans?

Another way, you can ask, why you are just Daniel and not your brother David?

The second part of this confinement problem is about the determination of first-person within all humans lived so far. This can be regarded as the "time and place" problem of first-person, which is:

From your first-person point of view, why or how, you are born in a definite "place and time"; and not any other "place and time" else? Simply, you can ask why you have just one life and why you are living here now in this time and in this place.

These two problems can be regarded as harder and the hardest problems of subjective consciousness respectively. However, these problems are very easy to apprehend if we do not make them complex. We are going to start with the second problem. Consider the first part of the 'confinement' problem—how it is determined which one would be you among all those living bodies. Suppose you are one of the identical twin siblings. You and your twin, both were born approximately at the same time and you both have roughly the same physical and genetic similarities. From your (the reader) point of view, you feel a first-person right now. You can feel pain, happiness, color, sound, touch and all those, which you think belongs to you only. However, those intimate feelings come from your body only and you know you are nothing but that materialistic body.

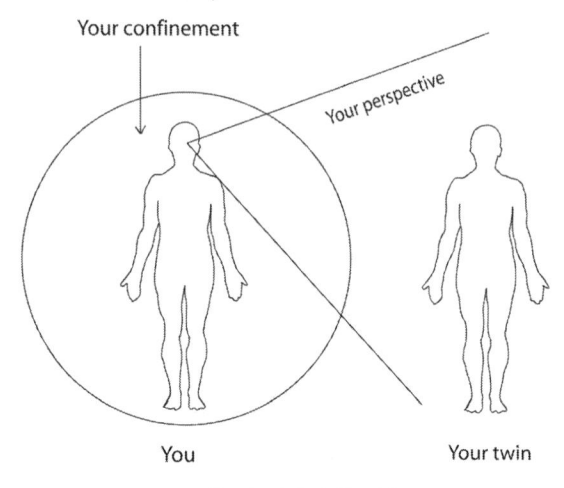

```
                    Your perspective
Your confinement
         ↓

       [figure: two body silhouettes, left one enclosed in a circle with lines indicating perspective from the head]

         You              Your twin
       One body is defined for you
              Fig: 3.5
```

Your twin also feels a first-person right now. He (meant no gender) is also nothing but his materialistic body. Two babies born at the same time from the same womb and you became just one of them. Which physical mechanism (laws of physics) on earth resisted you to catch the other body? What resists you to feel as the way your twin feels? You can feel your body subjectively, but you can never feel your twin's body the same way, though you know that your twin is also having subjective experience, same like you. It seems like your first-person is made for your specific body only, and it looks like it remains confined in your body as long as you live. How is this possible? How can you be just one of the identical bodies? You can only solve this problem by defining the fundamental differences between you and your twin's body. If you are John, and the younger of the twins, then why do you think you were left behind, at the time of your birth, from another same kind of human body? You may think, you are supposed to be one of the living human bodies and that is how you are just one of them random. Are you going to solve it this way? If you are, as usual, then consider the second part of the problem:

We usually think we have just one life. Why do we think that? Do we have any evidence of that thinking? Why do we use to believe that? Is it because our religion said so, or because of physicists and mathematicians don't have any idea about it? Whatever the truth is, if we really have just one life then there is a serious physical problem arise with that. Think about the time before you were born—1980, 1970, or 1955. If you are a theoretical physicist or a neuroscientist, interested in consciousness, then this 'thought experiment' has been specially designed for you. At the time before you were born, the universe was same like now, and the universal system created living things same like it is doing now. There were also billions of conscious humans feeling their first-person, at that time, same like you are feeling now. However, you were none within those humans. The laws of physics governed the universe at that time also, and there were neurobiological process created consciousness at that time also, so, why the universe could not create you at that time? Which exceptional condition of the universal system of that time failed to create you? Now think about the time after your death. There will be the same universe existing like now after your death, and there will be people living and feeling their first-person same, as you are feeling now, at that time also. Why you could not be created at that time? Why would all quantum and neurobiological mechanism fail to create your subjective consciousness at the time after you die? When the universe had the experience of creating your subjectivity for once, why could not the universal system create it again? What is the special condition of creating you as you are just for once? What is the cause that you can be created only at this specific time in a specific body, and no other time in other bodies? How your single lifespan is determined for this specific position and time?

Now you can see that your solution of the first part of the problem (confinement) is futile at this point. You are not supposed to be just one of the living humans randomly. You are one of the living humans within a certain period of living humans only. This problem instantly refutes all of our flawed concepts about consciousness. If consciousness (subjectivity) is an illusion created by the brain activity, then why hadn't you experience that illusion before you were born—when other people like you had been experiencing it firmly. If consciousness just comes from social and environmental correlation with our brain activities then why you can (each individual human) experience this process for a limited time only. Seems like you are absolutely unique with your first-person subjective consciousness from the others, as you cannot come anytime whenever humans live. There is a specific time allotted for you to be born and to live your life with others. If you are a neuroscientist or a cognitive philosopher and looking for a third-person method to show how your own subjective consciousness may arise from your brain, then it looks like your work area has been made limited by some unknown fundamental laws that physicists have not written down yet for you.

Still can't catch the problems? Relax, I also can't catch it always either because this problem is not a third-person collective problem. Everyone has to realize this with his or her own first-person consciousness separately. When we are trying to understand a problem of our own subjectivity, we must concentrate on our subjectivity and at the same time, we have to use our imaginations. That is why these problems sometimes may feel greasy. As both problems are closely connected to each other, let us go through the both problems simultaneously. There are seven billion other humans living with you in this world right now. They all feel the individual first - person same like you. They all, including you, are just the agents of creating first-person in this single materialistic universe. The whole universe is just a single system of existence (as it is supposed to be). Every matter, forces, and laws relate with every others in the universe and they all are fulfilling a common purpose collectively. When there is nothing outside of the universe and it is an existence, it must have its subjectivity to be self-recognized—as we have apprehended from the previous chapter, and when the universe is single it must have single subjectivity. If first-persons are just some subjective parts of the universe then all parts must be linked with each other subjectively. Just as like, when you have wounds on two different parts of your body, you feel pain from the both wounds at the same time, as all parts of your body is connected to nerves. Therefore, all first-persons should have only one common subjective point of view (perspective of experience) and from that single point of view, it should feel the pain of all first-persons collectively at the same time. But you know this doesn't happen in reality. You cannot feel other people's pain physically, whenever they hurt themselves, no matter how close you are to him or her physically and mentally. You may have your parents and children. You cannot feel any of their first-persons as 'you' either. However, they all possess different first-persons, and you are just one of them. Doesn't it seem like that you are occupying a specific but ordinary human body, from your birth time, in this world within many human races and generations?

Suppose, you were born in the year 1970, and you are going to die in the year 2070, you were born in the womb of a specific mother within the billions. You have acquired a human body. From your first-person perspective, you will remain confined in this body through your whole lifetime. Wherever you go, whatever you do you will never lose this intimate perspective of yours. You will feel and experience everything from the perspective of this body only. Our question is, why or how this lifetime, this specific womb and this physical body is determined for this perspective only by a physical law. If you were born for once and if your body came from the same quantum origin then where was this 'you' before you were born and where it will go after you die. Why weren't you born in the time of Christ or Pharaohs in another human body? How this body has been nominated for your experience only? After you die, the body must be degenerated and return to the physical elements like other dead bodies. What is so special about that ordinary materialistic body that it must be for you?

There are several points of arguments by which all physical laws can be questioned from your own viewpoint. First of all, you cannot deny that your specific first-person perspective is special for you. You know that an ordinary human body, which can create consciousness, has created your first-person perspective. But all other human bodies which can also create consciousness haven't created your first-person perspective. So which physical mechanism has made you unique among all those living humans?

Secondly, your first-person perspective did not appear before 1970, within all those conscious humans lived from the first humans on earth. So which physical mechanism blocked those conscious humans to attain your first-person perspective?

Thirdly, consider a universe with living humans where your first-person perspective never been created. Which order of God, or the laws of physics would be resisting your first-person perspective in that kind of universe? What mechanism ensures the certainty that your first-person perspective cannot be created at that imaginary universe? If our existing universe would have destroyed before 1970, your first-person perspective would never be created. But this is certain that your first-person perspective had the eligibility to come (as you are here now). How the physical laws of the universe that supposed to control the inception and annihilation of the universe can defend your first-person perspective to appear, when it (your subjectivity) has its hundred percent of eligibility to appear?

These are some distinct anomalies for any individual subjectivity from his or her individual first-person point of view. We cannot neglect it from a third-person (objective) perspective because there is no third-person perspective actually exists in this universe independent of first-person perspective. Anything in the universe must be experienced through first-person primarily, and no one can see the whole universe independently standing outside of it. Everything we understood or discovered so far, about this universe, came only through our first-person subjective reasoning. Albert Einstein apprehended the problem of light through his own first-person, same like these problems of first-person come through all individual first-persons—one of those is you. You can clearly see there is a separate 'you' exists within all humans in the world (present, past and future), and apparently there is no physical law exists for this 'you' to appear in this body, place and time. If even you think first-persons are separate 'souls' created by God, you can also seek for a mechanism of their (souls) distribution in a body, place and time.

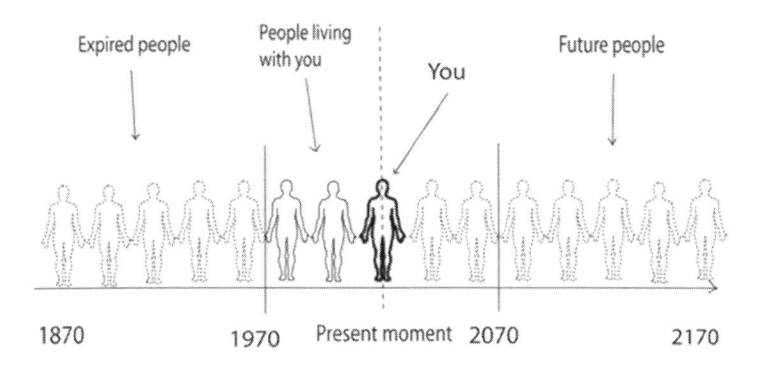

Specific time of individual first-person
Fig: 3.6

Now, do these seem some problems to you? Do these seem like intractable puzzles? If not, then I have nothing to say. If you are still going to chorus with those 'self-conscious' philosophers that consciousness can be explained using a third-person method from outside then I must doubt you are not a 'philosophical zombie'! If you think physics and mathematics would eventually solve these puzzles, then you are just over fascinated with physics and mathematics. Remember that we are here to understand the problem and to find a mechanism to solve the problem. If the problem is concrete then we must have to solve it before claiming a final theory of everything. However, these are only jigsaw puzzles according to the-I-theory; you just have to assemble the parts to know the answer. One thing is clear as crystal: **There must have been a fundamental system or mechanisms of the universe remaining that resists you to feel the**

pain of others and can make you appear at a specific time in a specific body. What is this mechanism that makes possible this apparent impossible is the greatest mystery has to be overcome by human knowledge before claiming that we understands everything in this universe. Unfortunately, we cannot solve this problem with our traditional observational science and by its physical theories known to us. But it has been declared by physicists that physics is already reaching its extremity with the M theory. So, no physical laws (laws of physics) won't be able to solve it even within a hundred billion years if it can't solve now. Searching the quantum and neurobiological mechanism of consciousness from outside will be useless to solve these physical problems of subjective consciousness. This problem of subjective consciousness must have to be solved subjectively— there is no fact other than this. Many of the scientists and philosophers do not want to consider their own subjective consciousness while they used to define consciousness. They used to account all subjectivity from a collective third-person viewpoint—as seemingly they can observe the universe from outside of it. However, individual subjectivity would have been, somewhat, insignificant if all of us would have borne with the first human and lived till the end of the world (it would have eliminated the problem of 'place and time' of first-person). When individuals come to live a limited life span, anytime anywhere, apparently leaving no trace behind, then cognitive scientists must take into account their own subjectivity in their research and start over.

We cannot even solve it with an omnipotent, omnipresent and omniscient God theory. Though the intentions of any traditional God are believed to be unpredictable, but if the laws of the universe have the least respect to a God (or vice versa), God must have been questioned righteously about placing a specific first-person at a specific place and time. If you think, God has created the universe by choosing strict and precise laws (like those supporters of 'intelligent design'). Even a God would fall in the same problem of superposition creating your subjectivity among the others. Do you need a proof of that? Consider that there are three identical blobs of fundamental particles A, B and C remains in front of God. God is going to create your subjectivity (first-person) within any of those blobs. How do you think he would decide which one would be you? From your subjective viewpoint, you will remain confined forever with that physique in which you will be created. Suppose, God wanted to give the C blob your subjectivity. So which law do you think he would apply not to give A and the B blob your subjectivity? Looks like God has nothing to do but choosing you randomly from those others.

So, which theory, do you think, is going to solve the problem of your first-person subjectivity? As a matter of fact, our existing theories do not even have a proper definition of first-person—what is it, how it can emerge guided by any physical laws of the universe. If a quantum fluctuation could give rise of the universe with no cause behind, then it seems a specific first-person perspective at any specific place and time is absolutely independent of any physical laws. If the universe would have destroyed before you were born then no laws of that universe could determine the certainty or uncertainty of appearing your first-person. Evidently, this cannot be happening—when you are here now, and it has been approved by your subjectivity. When every system is controlled by laws, then there must be a relation remains between the physical system of the universe and the appearing of your subjectivity at this specific place and time. In the next chapter, we shall step forward in the way of our quest for the origin of the universe by solving these riddles of subjective consciousness with a new physical mechanism—the mechanism so simple and accessible, and at the same time, so inevitable.

The way to immortality
(Solving subjective consciousness)

Anyone must realize that the problem of "position and time", explained in the preceding chapter, clearly indicates that the science of locality does not speak for subjective consciousness. From a strong logical standpoint, something must be apprehensible for you that when you were absolutely eligible to come with the first human body on earth (as there is no fundamental difference remains between your present body and the first conscious human body on earth) and apparently you did not, so there must be an ontologically fundamental mechanism remained which resisted you there. This is the most basic anomaly about subjectivity and consciousness; we must resolve this before exploring into the brain activity to see how consciousness actually works objectively. The-I-theory takes the attempt of solving this problem by defining "first-person subjectivity" not absolutely belongs to any individual person rather it fundamentally belongs to the universal existence. **In this sense, yes, you did come with the first human body on earth!** This may be harder to consume for many of us, but If we think that all "first-person subjectivity" remains painted on one universal canvas, then we do not need to find any other underlying mechanism for this anomaly. The key concept here is, human's subjectivity and personality (personal characteristic) are two separate qualities in a single body—personality is individual and subjectivity is universal. Our subjective qualitative aspects (qualia) like our raw feelings of pain and happiness, sensation of color, taste, sound are the same kind feelings distributed to all persons but fundamentally sensed from the universal perspective as a united feeling. This feeling represents the single subjectivity of the universal existence. However, on the other hand, our individual personality that separate us from the others, comes only from our stored memories, or from the experiences of our behavioral actions guided by our genetic formation and by other environmental and social correlations. In other words, personalities come from the preserved experiences stored as memories in the brain. But we need to understand that our first-person (physical subjective platform) does not preserve any experience; it just feels the present moment of time, like a sensor, on behalf of the universe and on behalf of individual persons (all individual persons belong to the universe). Thus, first-person with the help of consciousness (proper understanding) becomes individual, and feels itself as an individual person. First-person stays unchanged as long as a person lives with a sentient body, because first-person is just the extreme sensor of the universe that fulfills the criteria of true existence. So, our proposition is that the unique subjectivity of universal existence is the same 'thing' we feel as our own subjectivity. All humans feel the individuality of subjectivity as because they are all just different parts of the total existence, and that is why they cannot escape from this subjectivity. We know, experiences of humans are preserved in their brain as memories and in the genetic codes as instincts. Remaining aware with a physical body along at a stretch, catching continuously the present moment of time, and roaming freely in the memory-sets, first-person feels that it is alive and existed for a certain period of time that we call life. As a matter of fact, contrarily to our general belief, the-I-theory says that physically what is true existence is only first-person (with consciousness) in the whole universe, and it is created only to fulfill the primal inevitable condition of the universal existence. Objectively every other thing that our first-persons recognize as existence (except its own self) is just secondary existence existing in favor of first-person. The first person acts as a subject because it fulfills the self-recognition criteria of the universe and at the same time it is the primary recognizing agent of all objects that gives them (objects) existence. First-person is one, unique, free, everlasting, and it is recognizing everything from multiple subjective platforms on behalf of the total universal existence. These subjective platforms have remained distributed in all living things equally, and these have got vivid, reaching its extremity, at the conscious (understanding) level of humans.

Now it gets easy to think about a mechanism behind the "position and time" problem of subjective consciousness. If all subjectivities of humans are the same subjectivities they feel from different bodies, then there are no differences remained among those bodies. Therefore, why you were born in 1970, and not in 1870—**this problem will be partially solved if we just withdraw our belief of a single life span of humans.** If your specific first-person comes from the first humans maintaining a life and death sequence then it doesn't remain any difference of this present time with any previous or future time to your first-person. This solution may seem quite unorthodox compared to our traditional quest of understanding consciousness, but this is the only solution we can get through our all understanding capability for the problem of "position and time" of first-person. We can imagine a picture of this life and death sequence of humans, but this is not simply with separate columns of generations, as it may seem like. We have also our 'confinement' problem with living humans. Your parents and children may still live with you but they are all feeling different subjectivity. Beneath life and death sequence, there must be another deeper mechanism remaining here that makes this 'confinement' possible. So we must think about a single queue for all humans, orderly—one after another—from the first human to the last human child born. **It doesn't mean that at first there was just one human appeared on earth who remained at the top of the queue. There is an original mechanism of the fundamental system of the universe existed that resists catching multiple first-persons at the same moment of time and make humans come orderly—one after another.** So, your father and your son may not fall respectively the previous and next to you in this single queue. Within all living humans, there can be anyone previous and next to you, and which is determined by the fundamental universal system. This is the only way we can eliminate all differences among all human bodies regardless time in order to achieve a solution for both "position and time" and "confinement" problem.

As a review of the preceding discussion, we can say, subjectively, all human bodies are directly linked with each other in the fundamental level as the single subjectivity of the universe. Therefore, all subjective feelings of any individual human, including pain, are not absolutely owned by that specific human. Instead of those experiences in memories and genetic information—that creates our individual personalities—there is no other difference remains among all human bodies; different human beings living in different times are all the same persons feeling their subjectivity from different bodies only. Therefore, we can say, subjectively, there is just one human being living from the beginning until now in this world. In this context, what individual humans are feeling as 'pain' is unavoidable for them, and they are going to feel it ceaselessly as long as any human lives on earth. **Humans' physical death could not make them escape from this pain because the individual material-made bodies they possess are not the absolute authorities of their subjectivity. Any individual person living now will feel pain after his or her death from another living human body the same way.** This surprising fact reveals the secret of the 'life and death cycle' of human beings —we are going to explain this mechanism gradually in this chapter. But first we have to mention an another apparent anomaly in this solution.

Humans, fundamentally made of ordinary materials, feel inward subjectivity because first-persons or subjective platforms of the universe remain intensely exposed within them as long as their body remains aware. Continuity of proper consciousness (ability to understand systems) makes those first-persons feel like live. As the universe is single, so, in this context, there should be just one subjective perspective of experience for all living humans in the same physical time, and we are supposed to feel other living human's pain physically whenever they get hurt. But we know that it does not happen in reality. We all have our own separate perspectives of experience and we do not feel pain physically even from our closest ones. Here is the same fundamental mechanism of the universe resisting it—which makes all first-persons maintaining a sequence in time. Now what can be this unknown physical law of the universe that let us live our life with others without interfering in their first-persons? There is a matter of great surprise that we are already known of the mechanism that causes this physical confinement of first-person.

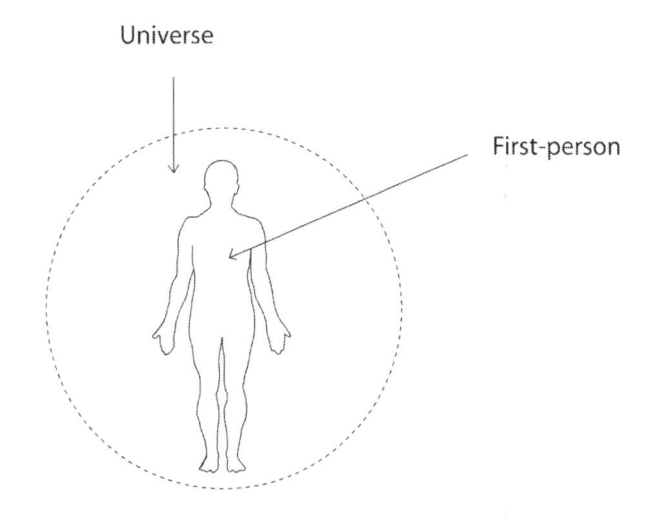

One first-person in the single universe
Fig: 3.7

This mechanism is widely established in the modern scientific community, and it is within the realm of quantum mechanics. We are going to discuss about this mechanism later in this chapter.

Now, we have found that first-person is a fundamental property of the universe and it is related to the grand reason of the origin of the universe. One of our fundamental questions was why first-person (subjectivity) does exist at all—now we are ready to give a logical explanation of this. When the universe had an inevitable condition to be self-recognized, subjectivity was compulsory as well as consciousness. The human body that obtained by evolution is just the perfect agent for this subjectivity among all nonliving and living things. That is why we have our subjectivity and that is why we have our consciousness. Our subjectivity with the help of our consciousness (understanding ability) recognizes ourselves so directly that it meets the criteria of self-recognition of the universe, and thus it gives the universe the satisfaction of true existence.

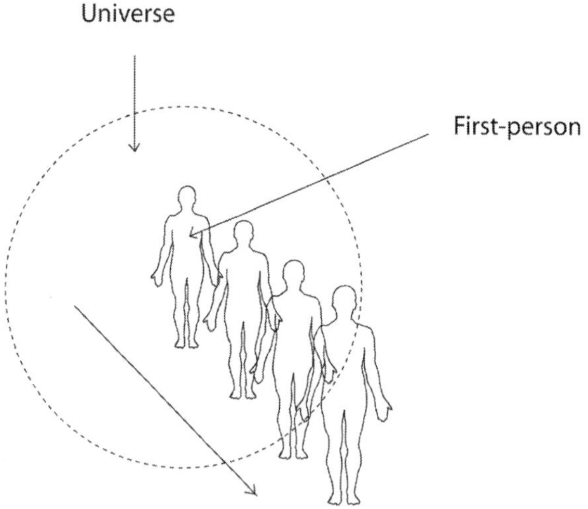

Single first-person seperated by life and death

Fig: 3.8

The existence of humans is also valued this way, but humans are more than just a self-recognizing agent because they all have their separate and individual personalities in which they remain confined until their death. Animals and other organisms, who mostly live their lives with the help of instincts, also have subjectivity but they do not have consciousness (proper understandings of the system) and imaginary power that is why they never feel themselves as individual persons like we humans do. Animals and other organisms do not have any confinement problem. This confinement has made human individual life valuable and meaningful. But, on the other hand, we share our subjectivity to all humans and organisms as this subjectivity is a universal feeling. What we feel as *qualia* is just the nonphysical feeling of existence of the universe itself acquired through human subjectivity (the renowned hard problem of consciousness is solved this way). Therefore, what we all feel as our 'self' is the self-feeling of the universe, according to the-I-theory.

From this logical conclusion, we can now go ahead formulating and proposing *the principle of universal self-existence* of the-I-theory as follows:

One and everlasting universal existence is fulfilling the inevitable condition of self-recognition, collectively, by the first-persons of human beings, creating and occupying orderly the very next point of consciousness, based upon fundamentally separate physical points of the universe.

This theory not only solves the hardest problems (position and time, and confinement problem) of subjective consciousness, it is also a self-sufficient ontological theory about the origin of the universe. Therefore, we can also entitle this theory as *the subjective cosmological principle.* Apparently, there are two separate sections of this theory. The first section resolves the 'origin' problem and the problem of "position and time" of first-person, and the second section resolves the first problem of subjective consciousness (restriction of transferring subjective information) or 'confinement' problem by explaining the mechanism how transmission of information amongst first-persons have been obstructed from the basic level of systems. Before we come to discuss this part, let us see how the first section of this theory comes in logical descending order:

1. Recognition or detection makes the difference between existence and nonexistence. Therefore, the condition of recognition is an inevitable condition for both existence and nonexistence.
2. Regarding the total existence and total nonexistence, we shall always get total existence when it is going to be recognized. Therefore, total nonexistence (nothingness) is impossible and total existence (universe) is absolute.
3. There can be nothing independent of the total existence; therefore, universal existence must have to be self-recognized to fulfill the inevitable condition. So subjectivity is a must for the universe.
4. Universal existence must have to be recognized by its own, so there must be something within the universe, which acts as a recognizing agent

on behalf of the universe.
5. When the recognizing agent is created by the universe itself, then it (agent) must always get subjective experience on behalf of the universe.
6. Only first-person subjective consciousness fulfills the criteria of self-recognition process, and humans fulfill the criteria of self-recognizing agents within the whole universe.

Therefore, the conclusion is, universal existence is fulfilling the inevitable condition of self-recognition by the first-persons of human being with a recognition process called first-person consciousness or subjective consciousness (without creating something like first-person consciousness and human beings, the universe could not have distinguished itself from nothingness).

Persuasively and reasonably, regarding the-I-theory, these are the logical premises behind consciousness. But the mechanism of achieving proper consciousness for a materialistic human body is far beyond these premises. We want to mention that anyone was ever thinking about any 'in depth' mechanism of consciousness so far objectively, keeping it under the apparatuses of neuroscience or psychology, underestimated consciousness remarkably. No one ever got any idea about a crucial fact that there are at least three essential mechanisms or functions remain for achieving consciousness for any materialistic body before consciousness becomes just a neurological function. These *set in* mechanisms are so vital for consciousness that these can abolish our hope of imitation of consciousness with man-made machines. These mechanisms can also answer all fallacies of intelligent design by describing the basic functions of consciousness. Following the principle of universal self-existence, the-I-theory formulates and proposes these mechanisms of first-person, which are fundamentally essential, and no materialistic body can achieve consciousness without maintaining these mechanisms. The mechanisms are as follows:

1. First-person was created by the energy of the universal existence (EUX) persuaded by the inevitable condition of the universal existence, **automatically** (blindly) achieving the appropriate laws of the universe.
2. In order to achieve consciousness, first-person is remained **somewhat free** from the binding of the physical laws from the moment it has been created (from the first living organisms).
3. First-person achieves consciousness from the collection of reflection of the universal system in the memories by enduring these reflections continuously **as time**.

Regarding the first essential mechanism, it is clear that the whole materialistic universal system, before any living organism created, had been a blind and automatic system regulated only to fulfill the inevitable condition. In this sense, this was not a mechanism at all; this was just an automatic function within the total mechanism from the inevitable condition to the consciousness. Before first living organisms, there was no conscious selection process occurred for any physical laws; all appropriate laws and precise parameters were just acquired automatically in favor of consciousness persuaded by the inevitable condition.

Second essential mechanism represents the second phase of universal development to achieve consciousness. This phase, started with the first living organisms, was totally different from the previous phase in mechanism, and there was no transition in between. This was really a blind leap of EUX from bindings to freedom. The energy of universal existence created a new kind of objects called organisms and **directly took over control** of them to give them life. EUX got 'the eye' with these sentient objects and started driving them almost freely coming out of the bindings of physical laws. That is how we have our free choices and that is how we have achieved consciousness. We wonder, why no one has ever mentioned that consciousness was impossible in hundred percent bindings of laws. If physical laws would have been regulated our all actions automatically then we would not have to remain aware about what we are doing or not doing, therefore, consciousness would have been futile.

The third mechanism says that consciousness comes from our concentrated thinking of any systems. Thinking is possible for us as we can roam in our memories. Memories are the nonphysical reflections of previous events stored in our brain. When we roam in the memories, we endure these reflections continuously, and this gives us the feeling of time. According to the-I-theory time is not a physical property of the universe; it is also not a "non-special" continuum where events occur from past to future direction"—what we have been taught by the theory of relativity. The-I-theory defines 'time' as an illusion of conscious mind, and this illusion comes from the conscious endurance of first-person within the previous reflections stored as memories. According to the-I-theory there is nothing called 'physical time' with respect to the universe, instead it (universe) is just changing its shape continuously remain in a single point forever. Only first-person consciousness catches this single point as the present moment of time—past and future is just created with our imaginations as we have our previous memories and as we can think about the future. This illusion of past, present and future, achieved by the endurance of continuous events as time, is an essential function for achieving consciousness.

Now the solution of the physical problems of "position and time" of first-person gets more clear from these essential mechanisms. The universe is remaining in a single point forever and continuously changing its shape with further events (from big bang to now, it is just continuous shape changing of the universe). There is just one human (the single subjectivity of the universe) here living forever, catching the present moment of the universe like a sensor, preserving the reflections in the memories and experiencing the illusion of time. This single human was divided into multiples in the first living humans created by the evolutionary process, and those first humans have lived until now just maintain a life and death cycle in a single order. Therefore, our hardest problem "position and time" is solved in this sense. There is no special time for any individual human. All humans living now are subjectively the same humans lived previously. Let us try to understand those problems properly from a detailed discussion:

How we recognize ourselves, and how we recognize the universe is the process of self-recognition for both the universe and us. Therefore, first-person stays at the zenith of existence. As we have mentioned earlier, If first person feels everything on behalf of the universe then there cannot be more than one first-person existed at the same time within the whole universe. If two first-persons exist at the same time then both first-person will be identical from both perspective of experience. If you are living with your twin at the same time then you both should feel the same pain and both should fall in a confusion of superposition. Physically you won't be able to decide which one is you when even you are physically separate from your twin. If you touch fire with your both hands, you will feel pain in both hands from your single brain. But in the case of universe there are no separate brain exits other than the human brain that creates the subjective experience of pain. So if two first-person exits, then any of those might feel the pain of the other. They also will not be able to understand their own identity and position because they are both feeling on behalf of the single universe from two separate brains only. So, only a single first-person can be existed within a single universe forever, fulfilling the condition of self-recognition. This is a restriction for first-person.

This is certain that the universe could not make consciousness (understanding process) this way, sustaining one first-person forever. Consciousness did not come so easily only guided by the laws of physics in ordinary living things. From the essential mechanisms of first-person, we can realize that first-person gets somewhat freed from the binding of physical laws and endured time continuously from the first living organisms to get consciousness. There were other thresholds, which had been achieved by evolution persistently. Starting more than three billion years ago and trying within more than ten million species at last just one species passed the genetic and physical threshold to get consciousness, which are humans. We know humans are not truly conscious without society and civilization. So just passing the physical thresholds was not enough for a living thing to catch consciousness. Therefore, the universal existence gives first-person the limitation of lifespan with death, or temporary destruction of first-person, and saves it from the problem of living at a stretch along eternity, and that is how it gets easier for first-person to catch consciousness.

Expired people

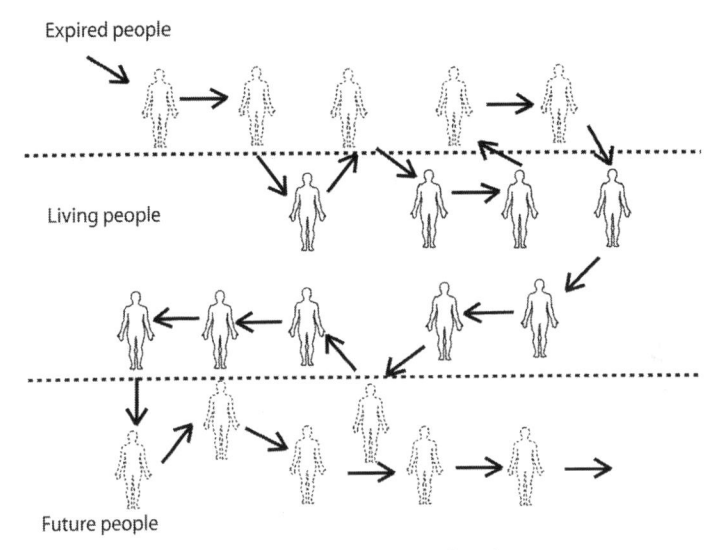

Living people

Future people

Point of consciousness maintaining a single order

Fig: 3.9

This clearly explains the solution of the physical problem of your first-person about position and time. How this specific time (your life) is defined for you here is not a puzzle at all. You have not just one life to live out, and you are not limited at this time only. You were always living from the first human and you will be living as the last human till the end of the world—only maintained by life after death sequence. You were in all human beings who already expired and you are in all living human beings who are living with you still now. You have passed all your life until now, and this time is the very present for the whole universal system that is why you are here now. This is not just one special time for you, which determined for you accidentally with no reason. But this explanation definitely doesn't answer the problem of our confinement from other individual first-persons—how the system determines which one will be you within twins, and how multiple humans are living together at the same time without interfering their subjectivities. The restriction of first-person confirms that there can be just one first-person existed in the universe, and not more than that is possible. But we know, we are billions of humans in this world living together. Every first-person seems to be independently feeling the same universe from their separate perspective at the same time. No first-person can switch to another first-person in reality though they are just the same feeling of the same universe. This is the confinement anomaly of first-person, which we marked earlier in this chapter. When you feel your pain, this is the most direct experience the universe could get through you. The universe gets the same experience of pain from another human. Both human's physical body and all feelings of pain belong to the universe, so why not you can feel the pain of another human, and why other humans cannot get yours, what separates your physical body to other humans within the same universe?

You may simply think that we are all physically separated humans; this is why we cannot feel each other's pain. If we could join two living human bodies with sensory nerves then both of them are going to feel the same pain—this is absolutely true. Conjoined twins can feel each other's pain if nerves of a shared limb remain connected to the both brains. They even could see through each other's eyes if all their optic nerves share the same optic chiasm in two closely attached brains. However, our problem is not with this at all. If we could join two or more human bodies physically with just one brain, then they must feel just one first-person as one body. So feeling each other's pain physically will not be unusual for them. We understood earlier that experiencing all bodied from just one first-person perspective is not implausible, instead, which unusual is the inability of feeling all bodies from any single first-person perspective. Our problem is with your (reader) first-person perspective only when you are one of the identical twins, and when you both have two separate brains. Obviously, both of you born, approximately, the same time, from the same womb, and both of you have physical and genetic similarities. When there is no known system to define which one should get your first-person, then both supposed to be getting your first-person (if you must have to get first-person within them). However, you identified your first-person as one of the twins, the other one always remains third-person to you, and you can never switch to the other. This could not be happening this way unless a fundamental mechanism of the universal system determines which one will be yours and which one not.

We have understood that every living being is fundamentally linked with each other—as they are within one universe, and all first-persons are just the sensory parts of the same universal existence. So, when all pain (or any subjective experience) is fundamentally felt by the universe, then if one living creature is hurt, all creatures should feel the same pain at the same time; but they don't. This is the fundamental problem of first-person comes after the solution of the problem of "position and time".

There can be just one solution of this problem and that is quite astonishing: the origins of all first-persons must be separated physically! According to The-I-theory, there are specifically five underlying facts remain as the mechanism of 'confinement' of first-person.

1. Every first-person (human) is created catching a unique physical point (a point of consciousness) of the universal existence.
2. The physical points, which catches individual first- persons are all physically separated (In-between gaps with nonexistence).
3. All first-persons come maintaining an order physically depending on those separate physical points of the universe.
4. First-person lives a non-physical life in a physical body.
5. Point of consciousness of first-person continuously develops over time according to the concurrent development of the universal system.

Regarding the first three facts, it is quite clear that subjectivity in a human body comes concentrated in a single point and which must be physical. Though our feeling of subjectivity and consciousness is purely nonphysical but the center-point of subjectivity that focuses on any system is a physical point of fundamental level, and it acts as an identity of first-person of organisms. We have termed these physical points as "point of consciousness", which are just fundamental quantum objects or quantum energy states. But when these points catch first-person or subjectivity these become the most glittering parts of the whole dark universe, and those are within the living organisms only. Our concept is, if all points of consciousness is not physically separated then all living things should feel each other's pain. So we need a non-physical gap between two points of consciousness that part the universal existence cannot sense subjectively. On the other hand, If all 'point of consciousness' of first-persons are physically separated but not created orderly, or created multiple at the same time, then our 'twin paradox' sustains—there will be no system to determine which one is going to be 'you' between twins. So if the universe has to create multiple first-persons then all points of consciousness must be remained separate physically (surrounded by nonexistence), and they all must come maintaining a single order, one at a time, to avoid interference of each other's subjective experience. Now that question arises, how can a single physical point be totally separated within the single universal existence where every point should be able to sense subjectively by the universe? Or, how can nothingness exist within things? However, we think we already know the answer, and, as you have been told earlier, the answer lies within the well-known theories of quantum reality.

From the mechanism of 'confinement', we have understood that first-persons are created by the single points or fundamental energy states of the universe and those points remain physically separated from each other. That means one single physical point can catch a single first-person on behalf of the single energy state of that point. So the very next energy state comes separately without transition destroying the previous one. This is how the transmission of energies happened, and this is how the universe develops in reality. This picture seems to violate the energy conservation law that says energy cannot be created or destroyed—but it doesn't, because the total amount of energy always remains the same here. At the quantum level, every object is created, and the next moment it vanishes to create the next one. This is how the energies can transmit as separate quanta at a time and not like a single wave. This is how we can make digital machines like computers. This digital transmission of energies is not random at all, it systematically follows the total development of the universe. The third fact behind the mechanism of our solution of confinement that says point of consciousness must come in a single order also represents quantum reality with the famous exclusion principle of Wolfgang Pauli; that is, two identical quantum objects (fermions) cannot occupy the same quantum energy state simultaneously. So there is no same moment of time for multiple quantum objects. For this reason, two first-persons from two points of consciousness cannot be created at the same moment of time occupying the same state of quantum energy level (this feature will be explained thoroughly in the expanded version of this book in the section "quantum subjectivity").

Now about the fourth and fifth facts of the mechanism of our solution and these are the most crucial of all; we know first-person has a life span with the life of living things—it doesn't just catch a physical point of the universe in a moment and destroys with the next moment. Life of a point of consciousness should be the smallest quantum time. So how a single first-person can live so long (the life of living things) and can feel everything from its confinement. The answer is, after it is created physically, the physical origin (point of consciousness) is destroyed immediately but the reflection of first-person remains preserved in the memory of the living things. At the next moment the following point of consciousness catches that previous reflection of first-person and thus it gives the continuity of consciousness to a specific living thing. So point of consciousness continuously develops with the development of the universe in a human body. These points of consciousness never interferes with the points of consciousness of other humans because of the isolating gaps. This is how confinement of first-person is created by the universal system. **In a simple sense, the fact is, in every quantum moment first-person of a human being is destroyed and created again at the next moment of quantum time. The very present quantum moment is always different to all**

living humans from the smallest level, so there is no same moment of time for all living-things that can cause interference of subjectivity. Point of consciousness of the present moment with the stored reflections (physical information) of previous points of consciousness creates a nonphysical 'bubble of consciousness' called 'self' in our memory. The bubble gets bigger or extends with time. The ceaseless continuity of consciousness we feel along our whole life is because of this bubble, which has directly nothing to do with your subjective experience. Only the point of consciousness of the present moment, which is strictly yours, senses your subjectivity (pain); you cannot share it with other organisms, and that is ensured by the universal system.

First-person lives within the memories of our brain and our living body sustains it until our death. There are several medical conditions like the state of coma, or brain dead situations in which first-person is eliminated. However, if the patient recovers from that condition and his memory remains intact, he feels first-person with the same personality again. Though first-person lives nonphysical life (except the very present point of time) but it cannot live without memories and without a living body. So it is just a 'self' or self-consciousness, not anything like a soul, which thought to be fly around without a living body.

So when the development of the universal system is separated physically with different energy states, no one can originate at the same point (energy state) of the universe with another. So not only have we order in generations in which we are born, all humans living with us are in another different single order separated by physical systems of the universe. This physical points or energy states are originally the base of our focus of mind, or concentration. All our memories start from this physical point a time long before our birth and carried away as long as we live. This is the point, which feels our first-person on behalf of the whole universe, and it has no transition with its previous and succeeding points. This is the energy point, which has free will, which persuades and persists for all our understanding and consciousness. Practically and sensibly, according The-I-theory, this is the underlying mechanism by which you feel that you are living here at this time, reading the book remaining confined in your first-person, as a separate person all independent of this materialistic world.

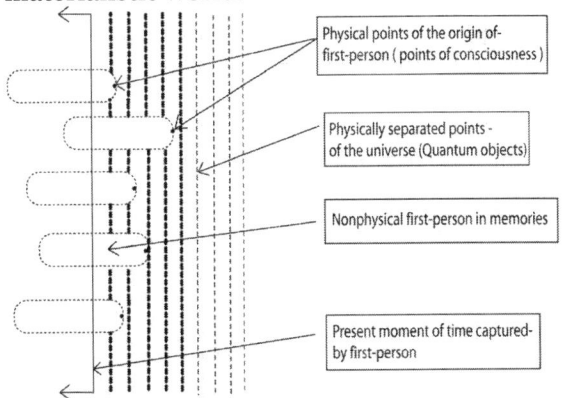

Physical points of the origin of first-person (points of consciousness)

Physically separated points of the universe (Quantum objects)

Nonphysical first-person in memories

Present moment of time captured by first-person

Nonphysical life of first-person with physical origin

Fig: 3.10

Now the most interesting part—**what is going to happen after you die**—though the answer is not quite interesting as you may expect. You are living now, you have your direct perspective of experience, you have your distinguishable personality that you acquired through your life. After you die, your personality will be destroyed with the destruction of your memory and body. After you die, your body will fail to catch the continuation of point of consciousness that created your subjectivity. But you know other people will also live after your death. If all subjectivities are the same then you will must live after you die. But how would that happen. You can think that you are going to catch another point of consciousness with a new born baby and start a new life again immediately after you die.

But this is not the way it would be—you are not going to switch. After you die, your personality is not going to shift or transfer to another person's body, or in a new body but you will remain exist this is for sure. We have understood that here are differences between personality and subjectivity. Our personality is created by the experiences in our memories, instincts and genetic information; it varies with each person. But subjectivity is the raw feeling that we get physically, and it is the same feeling to everyone. Your personality is unique and special to you but your subjectivity is nothing special. You are a direct observer from your perspective and the same way other peoples are the direct observer from their own separate perspective. How you feel as your existence is the same feeling to other living humans at the same time. You are just one perspective among billions. **As a matter of fact, other peoples are also 'you' from other perspectives.** So, when you will die your (reader) specific perspective will vanish only, your direct observation will continue from other perspectives (which are also yours subjectively) with other people. You will live after your death same like you are living now. There is no system to determine which one will be you after your death because there is no physical or intellectually detectable event happens except the destruction of a specific personality. We can easily understand it from a couple of 'thought experiment': suppose there are only two persons living in the whole universe. One is you in a dying planet and the other is in a hospitable planet far away a galaxy apart. Fortunately, you know that there are only two people exist in the whole universe and you know the theory that subjectively you both are the same persons. You kill yourself to be the other one. What do you think would happen? Nothing, you won't feel that you have switched to the other person in the other planet because there are already another 'you' living with another personality. So there is nothing to switch between two 'you', but one thing is sure that you will still be lived as that living person. Things will get more complicated when we shall take three or more people. There is no way you can have an idea how and where you are going to live after you die when there are more than two people living. Although this is very much clear that you are going to live within the living people and at the present time after your death—you are not going to miss any moment of time as long as any human lives in the universe. Now you (reader) can easily solve all of your problems regarding your existence. Why you exist? Because your existence fulfills the existence of the universe, so your existence is unavoidable. Why you are here, it is because his is the present moment of time of the universe and you are always living in the present moment. Why you are confined in John (reader) and not anyone around you? It is because you represent some unique moments with your points of consciousness, which you cannot share with others.

Why you are living now in the twenty-first century and not in the time of the Pharaohs—this question is absurd now because indeed you were at the time of Pharaohs. Precisely, you are all living and expired humans. Subjectively you were Pharaoh and you were Moses, you were Jesus and you were also Judas, you were Hitler and you were Gandhi. Though, as a person, they were all different as they had their separate personality depending on their individual perspective of experience.

What is going to happen after you die? The answer is, you are not going to die. As long as any human lives in the universe, you will live. The floating 'bubble of consciousness' of yours is dependent on the universe and other way it is independent as it is strictly yours. You will always find a ready-made universe for you along eternity. This is how you will live your 'single' life within your immortality.

The inevitable theory explains what first-person really is, why it exists in a physical universe and how it exists. The surprising conclusion of this theory is that the first-person we feel is the same feeling to all humans. We all may be different persons but what we feel as pain is the same thing for all humans. Our individual personality belongs to us, but what we feel subjectively is universal. We are just agents of this first-person developed in a systematic process through cosmological development and biological evolutions having the satisfaction of our life and the same time giving the universe the fulfillment of its existence. Definitely, we can never die! To say precisely, our first-person never dies with our death. Our death just destroys our body, our memories and associated personality, but we shall feel the same pain through another human body after our death as the pain and all physical feelings we get, is separate from our personality. Though our first-person is not going to die, there is nothing to think about that we are going to born again. When we die first-person just loses one body, or the body just loses the capability of holding a first-person and it remains in all other living bodies. There is nothing to calculate if anyone is going to be a prince or a popper after he or she dies, and there is no scope of thinking of any 'incarnation' or avatar or traditional life-after-death concept within this mechanism.

Therefore, this is clear that you are not going to miss any physical time and place where a human lives. You are going to live in the present time after you die, and this system will continue as long as the world or the universe has the environment suitable for life. Your position here in this body or your fixed life span, from your birth time, is nothing so special. You must always remain with a physical body, and this is the present moment of the physical universe, that is why you are here now. You have seen the cave life of humans physically and you will certainly witness the end of the world remaining physically at that time. There is no escape for you from this reality.

One other thing has to be made clear here that the universe does not feel all the first-persons of human beings from a different and single perspective of its own. The universe has no separate 'first-person' except within humans. The universe does not feel more than what we do, or, we can say, this is the best the universe can feel as an existence just what we feel as a living being. We can consider the whole universe including us is just one body of a system. When the universe sees through us, then we are the eyes of the universe, when it thinks through us, then we are the mind of the universe, and when the universe lives through us, we are the heart of the universe. We can say, in the other way, that the first-person consciousness is the nonphysical 'thing' that 'feels' the universe as its own systematic and physical base. The first-person not only belongs to the universe, the universe also belongs to first-person. So we can surely ask which comes first, first person or the universe. The answer is surprising; both came at the same time! In need of existence, both are absolutely depending on each other. In the previous chapter, we intentionally mentioned that self-recognition is the prior condition of the universe, but question of recognition of anything must come after the existence of that thing. In this stage, the concept of self-recognition gets clear to us, that is, the existence of the universe and self-recognition both comes exactly the same moment of time, not prior or after. We can think, tables and chairs will remain as it is here, even if there are no living things—this is our typical materialistic worldview. However, if there is no first-person exists to recognize those objects, then they are definitely nonexistent. If the universe remains billions of years without first-person, it would just remain as nonexistence because no one would get the information of that kind of universe anyway. This is not just a conceptual theory; this is true reality. Eastern poet and philosopher Rabindranath Tagore argued with Albert Einstein, at this point, at a meeting in New York in 1930. At that time, they did not understand that they both were right. Objects will remain, as it is, if there is no first-person consciousness to recognize them. But these will remain in nonexistence phase, no matter how long these remain in that phase, and when they want to come into existence again, they must come through the process of recognition creating first-person consciousness with the same kind of humans like us. Objects have no other choice to become existed other than self-recognition. So, we can propose, a recognizing agent recognizes itself and the objective universe, at the same moment of time, to come into existence. Conscious humans and the universe were born at the same moment of time. Unbelievable? Believe it!

The universe and time

Did the universe start from a single point with a Big bang? Observing the expansion of the universe and cosmic microwave background scenario we make ourselves believe this. Whatever the mechanism of the starting point (if there was a starting point at all), the universe could not start without a cause. The-I-theory explains the inevitable condition that the universe could not help starting when this condition acted in the first place. Cosmologists have calculated, approximately, fourteen and a half billion years have passed from the starting point of the universe. The scientists also used to tell us why we should not ask such questions like: why the universe did not start before that period, or what unusual thing happened at that time that a universe should have to start? Scientists suggest that *time* starts with the starting point of the universe, so, if there was no time before that period then there was no 'before' exists. Quite a strong rational sense is needed to understand this fact that philosopher as Immanuel Kant failed.

However, we already know that the-I-theory says, time did not start with the starting point of the universe and, as a matter of fact, it never started physically. Only an illusion of time started with the first emerging of consciousness in human beings (let alone other living organisms). Before consciousness emerged, the universe remained in the same moment like it was at the starting point because there was no one or nothing to compare that phase with the starting point. At that period, only what remained in the universe is motion. If we could observe that period from a third-person point of view from the outside of the universe then we would see that the universe was changing its shape continuously—like a jellyfish—remaining at the same point forever. The universe is still remaining at the same starting point that we call 'present'—just changing its shape continuously. Does it need much rational sense to understand?

We always had some misconceptions with time and its characteristics. Albert Einstein fired up these misconceptions introducing outstanding concepts of fourth dimension, time dilation, and time travelling. People, nowadays, do not really want to know what the Bible or the Quran or others say about time, because Einstein already told about it. But do we really understand what Einstein said about time and its characteristics? Was time a physical thing or physical property of the universe according to Einstein?

What we have in the universe is the motions of mater and energies only. The event created by those mater and energies that is only physical, and time is just a feeling of persistence that is strictly belongs to living things, especially, humans. We see, everything is continuously changing within the universe. There is nothing that can be absolutely static, all are relatively remains in motion. That is why we have a feeling of time in our mind relative to all these motions. Yes, time is just a conscious feeling of living things; time is not a physical dimension of mater and energies that can be dilated or can be stretched physically. On the other hand, motions of mater and energies can be slower or faster in certain situations and thus the interval between events can be slowed or hurried—this doesn't mean that time 'itself' has its physical flexibility. So, where this 'spirit' called time lives? It lives only in our memories!

Let us recall the third essential mechanism of first-person consciousness we proposed in the previous chapter, **"First-person achieves consciousness from the collection of reflection of the universal system in the memories of living things by enduring these reflections continuously as time."** This is exactly how first-person lives. When various motions of the universe are sensed by the first-person through sensory organs of living things, the reflection of those motions captured and stored as memories in the brain, and persisting on these memories continuously, first-person gets the feeling of time. So, the feeling of time is a crucial factor for consciousness. Let us take a look at the figure in the following page:

Fig: 4.1

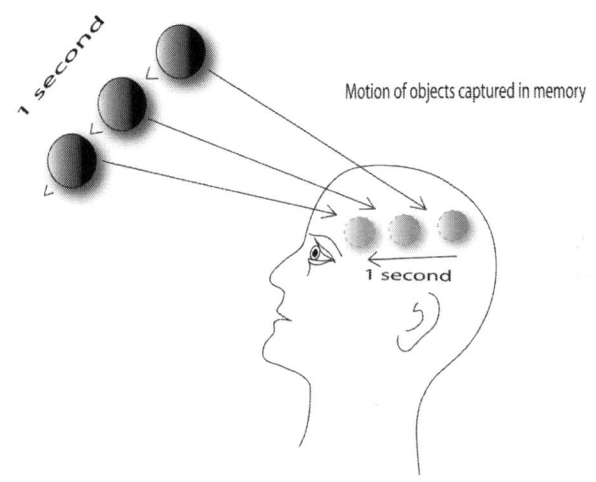

First-person experience of motion and time

Motion of objects captured in memory

We know that time always expressed in a way of motion to us. Earth's spin on its own axis, moon's travelling around the earth, earth moving round the sun is the cosmic motions we observe every day. Earth's spin gives us the most practical experience of time. We understand time from observing our physical growth, the growth of plants, decaying of materials. Observing all those motions altogether we feel that time is 'something' and that is passing by continuously, along with the universe.

Now consider that you do not have the ability to store anything in your memory. How could you locate that there is motion all around you or changes of everything is happening? Even if you have a sensor like first-person, which can catch the reflection of present motion of the universe, but if you do not store it continuously and orderly anywhere and cannot recall it, you will not get any information about the previous state of anything. Therefore, in this case, you won't locate any change of anything, you won't get conscious of motions or events, and you won't feel anything that we call time.

We can clearly understand this condition with a simple 'thought experiment'. Consider you have acquired an unusual disorder of the brain. We can name it Charlie Chaplin movie disorder. As a symptom of this, you cannot store continuous memory like normal people. You just miss one second after one second of the information of present motion in your memory. What will be your experience of time? You will certainly see that everything in the world is going faster, including the dials of a clock. You would be experiencing like watching Charlie Chaplin's silent movies in real life. In this situation, your personal feeling of time will be different from normal people. Some people remain in a coma from a medical condition, like head injury, and this condition can eliminate their consciousness for a long time, sometimes for a year or more. If they can make themselves recover from that condition, they remember that the incident (head injury) happened in just some moments ago. The whole one year of time just lost from their memories. So we can see that the feeling of time dwells absolutely within our memories. The experience of time comes only from the endurance in our memory—the endurance of motion of objects, and the endurance of interval of events. This endurance of time gives us consciousness, give us understanding and give us life.

We used to think that time makes the decaying of materials and objects. But, actually, the reality comes from the opposite direction—observing decaying of materials gives us the feeling of time. There is nothing wrong if one of a twin travels in a situation where his physical growth delays for environmental reason and he remains younger, but that doesn't' mean time was stretched to him in that situation.

There are genetic disorders of accelerated aging called Progeria, where the patient's cells grow faster than normal people's cells, so the patient grows older very fast and dies as an old man in his teen or preteen age. This is due to genetic dysfunction of faster than normal metabolism of their cells only, not due to the contraction of time. They (patients of Progeria) definitely do not feel time faster goes around them; there can be no separate time allowed for them within normal time. So why do we think there are some extreme situations when or where time is contracted or stretched. This is because we think time is a physical property of the universe. There can be special situations due to gravity and speed where the normal motion of quantum objects can be slower, metabolism of cells of human's can be slower, but that situation will be nothing to do with the feeling of time of conscious humans; humans won't feel any change of time anywhere in any situations in the Universe.

We have some other scientifically featured misconceptions about the arrow of time. Why do you only remember the past and not the future—this is a question originated from these misconceptions. The-I-theory suggests that there is no mental arrow of time exist other than the way the universal system develops or changes. In the case of C, P, T violations, we think when T is violated (changing the direction of time) we will see that everything is running backwards; broken cups will jump up from the floor onto table getting one piece again, smoke will run backwards into the chimney, even dead will come alive from graves. But this is just our imagination. Altering the direction of time won't work if the direction of all forces is not altered. In that case, gravity, electromagnetic, and strong nuclear force would be repulsive forces and that would just cause the destruction of the universe—not running time backwards. Another thing is, if we do not stop the whole universe at a point first, we cannot make the T violated—even hypothetically. And when all motions of the universe will stop at a point, consciousness will stop immediately. Your continuous capturing of information of the motions will be stopped also, and when all the motions will run backward, a human will lose its memories continuously. He or she will not be able to experience anything because of his or her continuous loss of memory. The inventor of a time machine, intend to go to the past , will fall in the same situation of memory loss and at the same time will also lose his own time machine that's supposed to make the universe stand still and run backwards. If we still think we would be able to observe that time running backwards, we won't start remembering the future. Whatever action occurs in the universe in any direction

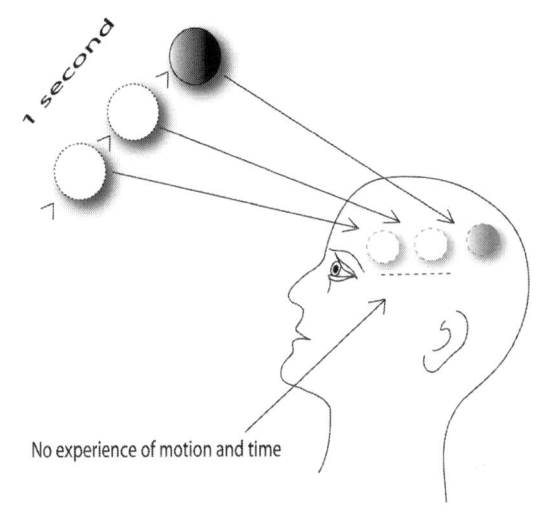

No experience of motion and time

Time and motion of objects is not possible to experience when T is violeted (Time runs backwards)

Fig: 4.2

humans will catch it as present and store its nonphysical reflection as past, future will always remain undetermined and uncertain.

Which system do you think preserves the previous information of motion in this universe other than humans do in their memories? We know light preserves physical information of all materials, motions and events. But which can recall this information? If no one can recall it except humans then no one feels anything like time except humans. Our first-person resides in our memory and gets the endurance of time simply by comparing all present motion with the information of previous motions—thus all living things live in an illusion of time. Time is nothing more than that. Time is not a 'ghost' that comes from the starting point of the universe and stays head-to-head with space. However, we know 'time dilation' is a proven fact, but this is only about changes in frequencies of light and other radiations and changes in quantum motions due to the speed of objects and due to gravity. There is no relation of this mechanism with what we call time except in views only (the true mechanism of time dilation will be explained in the expanded version of this book).

This fourteen and a half billion years, including the starting point, is just one single state of the universe in motion, only the present moment of physical change is caught by human consciousness (first-person) and stores in the memories. So, we can say, the universe remains at the same point forever but changes continuously in timelessness. The universe may have a starting point, but it is nothing different from the present moment of the universe, except variance in total shapes. According to the-I-theory, coming to a specific shape the universe creates consciousness and fulfills the condition of existence. Before consciousness or first-person, no universe could meet the criteria of existence, practically or hypothetically, no matter which initial condition it maintains. Therefore our conclusion is, the universe and first-person came at the same moment in existence creating the illusion of time in human perceptions.

So, how can we think of a model of the universe without time? Some physicists, including Stephen Hawking, do not want to consider an idealistic theory for the explanation of the origin of the universe, especially where humans remain as a prime factor of origin. The only reason they show that these tiny living creatures on an average rocky planet, inhabiting in an average solar system of a typical spiral galaxy are very much insignificant compared with the unimaginable abundance of the universe. The universe is for humans—they can't just believe it. The universe is unimaginably vast, there is no doubt about it; and it is full of countless colossal objects like planets, stars, galaxies, quasars. These objects live billions of years. Compared to them, the size and lifetime of human's are indeed insignificant. But what confirmed us that the priority or importance should come in physically descending order from bigger to smaller, from stronger to weaker. We don't really see this in our reality. We know, only four forces are responsible for this abundance of the universe, and the strongest of those remains at the smallest level of matters. Nuclear fusion starts from the atomic level and can ignite a star. Even the universe is thought to be started from a tiny point, which was unimaginable small in size. So, evidently, everything is controlled from the smallest level. Size doesn't determine everything in this universe. Another thing is, just one galaxy does not suffice for developing conscious beings. We humans have already proved it by asking about the boundary condition of the apparent infinite universe. When light must go in straight lines, it can be proved logically that an infinite universe is needed for consciousness even if there may be only one planet is existing with intelligent beings within the whole universe. We know that we humans are in a position roughly the same distance from the stars and from the atoms. This our favorable physical size that let us remain stable and safe on this planet after 3.7 billion years of biological evolution along with twelve thousand years of civilization for perfect consciousness.

However, we have seen that Professor Stephen Hawking in his book *a brief history of time* reluctantly suggested the 'strong' version of *the anthropic principle* for solving various fundamental problems including how the variations of parameters of the universe had been chosen initially. Anthropic principle or anthropic cosmological principle, especially the weak version of it, and hypotheses like *biocentrism* is somewhat related with the-I-theory, however, these can be proved incomplete as a cosmological theory in at least three different ways. We would like to mention this here because we need to distinguish the-I-theory not only as an idealistic theory but also as a complete cosmological theory. First of all, for the anthropic principle, it doesn't answer why the universe needs something tiny like these living organisms and intelligent humans while giant and supergiant nonliving things actually reign in this universe. Secondly, it does not attempt to explain the mechanism of human subjective consciousness in view of its problems of 'confinement' and 'position and time'; and, finally, it does not indicate any initial cause of the emerging of the universe. A hypothetical 'multiverse' concept have been craftily suggested in the strong anthropic principle, but we know, this concept is one of the greatest violations of Occam's razor, and it is nothing but a *sci-fi* solution of the problem of the existence of the universe; let us see how:

The-I-theory applies an inevitable condition for the universe that it must have to be self-recognized to come into existence. This is certain that somehow it fulfilled this condition—as we can recognize it now. We understand that a certain initial condition, necessary characterization of forces (laws) and precise variation in cosmological parameters made this possible. Therefore, what we see as the condition of the universe now, it certifies the certainty of its existence. Any variation in parameters other than this, which cannot create consciousness, must remain the universe in nonexistence phases, and therefore those variations were simply impossible to catch for the universe. The universe inevitably caught the precise variations simply rejecting all improbable to reach a certain destination. Therefore, we don't need to consider any other variations than these certain variations of the universe. One may think that the universe would have come choosing this variation in parameters from the infinite amount of parameters, but dealing with infinity is sometimes harder than we can imagine. If the universe would have chosen the right variations from the infinite amount of variations then there was always a fifty-fifty chance remained for the universe of finding the right ones. In a series of infinite variations, there is always a fifty-percent possibility of finding it any time and there is a fifty-percent possibility of never finding it—and just keeps searching forever. Definitely, you would agree that the universe we see here did not come with only a fifty-percent certainty. What really happened here was that the preexisting inevitable condition directly caught the right universe; other infinite amount of universes, which was implausible in favor of consciousness, could not come into existence.

We can see here how the universe caught the consciousness developing itself automatically by cancelling the unnecessary variations. There was no scope of any supernatural or intelligent involvement in this process, and there was no conscious choosing happened (with free will) before the first living organisms emerged. That means, 'the watchmaker' was truly blind before biological evolution started! This is bad news for 'intelligent designers' and theologians. On the other hand, no living organisms before humans were truly conscious. Primordial organisms conducted their lives mainly by instincts, instructed by information preserved in their genes. Instincts are also regulated by the energy of the universal existence (EUX) as a persisting collective force, which created the whole universe and at last became conscious and intelligent through the process of evolution. What we call intelligence or proper understanding with consciousness comes with the humans only. Animals also have their endurance of time in their memories but they are not truly conscious like humans because of their incapability of thinking and understanding perfectly. They don't feel themselves as persons; so their 'confinement' is not like us. So what it is like to be an adult animal is nothing more than like an 'aged infant', who cannot think properly and stays alive mainly with the help of instincts. Although animals have their endurance of time but they cannot recall it like humans. What we call confinement of subjective consciousness belongs to humans only.

We see subjective consciousness plays the prime role in cosmological theater. So what should be a model of the universe involving subjective consciousness from the fundamental level? Before thinking of a complete cosmological model of the universe with the help of the-I-theory that can be regarded as **the subjective cosmological model** (described in the expanded version), we can make a very simple but effective idea of it.

Suppose that you were remaining as a 'concept' of universal existence in the total nothingness. This total nothingness had been inhospitable for you. You felt that you were remaining submersed in an infinite ocean holding your breathe. You didn't find a place or air where you could take your breath. If this 'breathing' acted as an inevitable condition for you that anyhow, you must breathe, then it must be induced an energy within you. Suppose you could do anything with this energy. You built a hollow place within that endless ocean and filled it with air. Then you wanted to raise your nose within the air bubble and took your breath, but there was nothing where you could stand, or what could support you for long. So you built a platform or a base for standing at the edge of the air bubble, and you kept creating bases all the way down to make it sustaining for a certain time. You gave the base a perpetual form so that if it destroys in a level, it could create the level automatically. That was how you found a chance to take your breathe standing on the top platform. If, somehow, the whole system collapsed, you would fall in the previous situation of holding breathe, where your inevitable condition still remained, so your energy would induce again. If that 'breathtaking' condition was associated with your consciousness then you would always find that you were taking breath in an air bubble no matter how long it was taken to create, or how many times it was destroyed in the process.

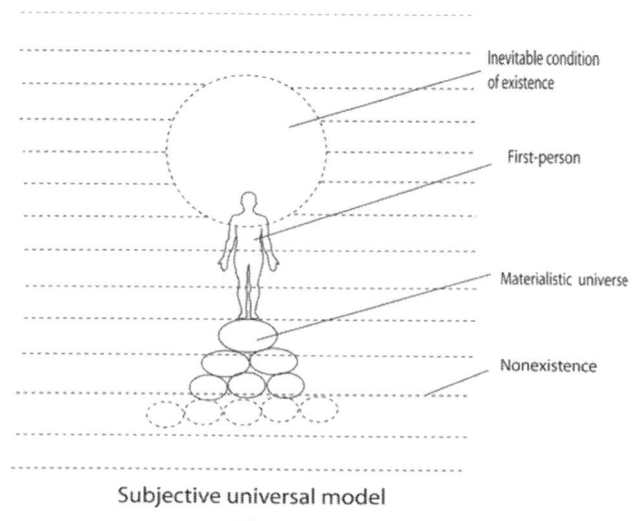

Subjective universal model

Fig: 4.3

Figuratively, the same thing happened here for both the universe and us. We can make any detailed cosmological model of the universe easily from this insight. One of the probabilistic models (supported by the-I-theory) has been proposed in the expanded version of this book as a complete and independent model that can cope with all our empirical observations including the cosmic microwave background radiation and the expansion of the universe smoothly. Whatever the explicit model of the universe that includes the origin and consciousness, the-I-theory confirms, it must have to be inferred from our pretty little figurative one, and we think that has just enough 'ideals' to understand the scenario perfectly. This simple figure can solve many puzzles about the existence of the universe. This model certainly differs from our traditional world-view, but this is the reality, behind the curtain, that always keeps us in enigma when we try to understand the fundamental reasons. However, by the way, doesn't it seem like the tortoise after tortoise model of that old lady, who was somewhat annoyed after being lectured by a renowned scientist? If it does, then this is just a coincidence.

Paradox of freewill

Do we have freewill? "No, we haven't", says the physicist. "The universe is guided by the laws of physics and nothing can act independently denying those laws—not even our conscious choices". Some philosophers say another thing, "The universe is not all deterministic, and we certainly have our freewill within various constraints of nature." In philosophy, the argument is all concern of determinism and libertarianism. Libertarians, who want to give a chance to free will, do not think that the universe is all deterministic, while on the other hand, there is no place for free will in hard determinism. There also have been long, unsolved, ambiguous debates going on within compatibilists who says free will is logically compatible with the deterministic universe, and incompatibilists who says exactly the opposite. Nevertheless, the-I-theory clearly suggests that we have our choices; we are not programmed robots or 'philosophical zombies'. As an essential property of first-person, we have learnt: **first-person was created by the systematic laws of the universe, and it was freed from the bindings of laws from the moment it was created (from the first living organisms).**

So, which of the statements is true? Do we have freewill or not?

One thing is very much sure that pledging freewill with logic and commonsense is extremely difficult. We always feel that we are the authority of our conscious decisions, but thinking deeply about the natural systems give us negative vows about that freedom. If we consider that this is only a systematic universe guided by rigid laws of physics, no scope for impulsions and choices, then the physicist is right. In the universe, no single system is fully independent; every system is related to every other system. In the universe, there has a cause behind every action and these actions also acts as a cause of further actions. So each action in the universe is triggered by a cause before it. There has a cause before any movements in our body, behind our breathing, our metabolism, our blood circulation, in our cells, and even behind the thinking process in our brain. The continuous electric movement (brain waves) in our brain conducts our continuous thinking process. We are forced to think flawlessly as long as we remain conscious. Our brain cannot stop thinking and remain blank for even a second. As far as we concern, electrons systematically hit a specific memory function, and that specific memory function gets the priority in the thinking process. Our sensory organs catch the experiences of our actions with the outer environment. Certain experience creates certain chemical changes in our body, and the information of all these chemical functions remains stored in our memory. By the influence of those stored experiences, our brain knows what to take as a priority in thinking in new situations. This priority defines our decisions among so many constraints or choices created by the universal system. So there always must have a predominant cause behind your every decision in every moment. All the origins of these predominant causes systematically come from the origin of the universe (if this is just a deterministic universe). So, seems like you just live your life permitted or limited by the universal system. You are all destined by the universal system; you have no choice except to let it happen as it is going to be. So, definitely, you do not supposed to have any free will of yours. If all your acts are driven by the systems of the universe independent of your will, technically, you should not be rewarded for your good deeds, and you should not be punished for your offenses!

However, this could be only the case of an all deterministic universe. Now we have, experimentally supported, quantum theories, based upon uncertain or the probabilistic nature of subatomic particles, which indicate nothing but casual indeterminism. The famous double slit experiment suggests that individual fundamental particles can have more than one possible course of action at the same moment of time, therefore, the future of those particles always remain unpredictable. We humans often face dilemmas where we can be forced to take more than one decision at the same time. Contemporary philosophers of metaphysical libertarianism believe that this natural ability of humans is something to do with the uncertainties of the fundamental level. But unfortunately we do not have reliable theories so far that can merge free will with an indeterministic universe. Supporters of freewill cannot say how an agent can act independently ignoring the laws, or how can it act by taking advantage on the uncertain nature of subatomic particles. We, at least, do not have theories that can logically prove us that we have our free will. However, the-I-theory settles all these problems in one hand. The position regarding free will is very clear in the-I-theory. It says, human ability of conscious choices is not an illusion, and it can be proved, at least, logically. On the other hand, very surprisingly, the-I-theory does not support any physical uncertainty and randomness within the universal systems, not even in the fundamental levels. It suggests that subatomic particles have just one possible course of action permitted by the system. (Please do no grin so early if you are so convinced with uncertainty principle and double slit experiments. We do not mean to deny Heisenberg and Young at all; this is not in contrast with the facts observed in the fundamental level, this is just in contrast with the apprehension of the facts.) For this moment, we are not coming up with the old argument that says, physical uncertainty and randomness cannot ensure the stability of any system of any moment. In the respect of free will, the-I-theory only alters the methodical aspects between quantum uncertainty and human conscious choices, and this would definitely change our worldview and solve all mysteries about quantum uncertainty. As an essential ingredient of first-person consciousness the-I-theory suggests that only first-person, within the whole universe, can deny the physical laws and drive its 'belonging agents' (e.g., humans) purposefully with efforts. One thing we have to keep in mind that unlike Descartes 'dualism' the-I-theory considers first-person as an inevitably achieved **true state of existence,** and not a thing or entity, which lives in the mind. According to the-I-theory this true existence or 'bubble of consciousness' is the nonphysical authority that ensures (with recognition process) the existence of everything in the universe. When this' Bubble of consciousness' or first-person is inevitably achieved by the physical system, it must have its certainty of achievement with a set of physical laws which only gives certain results, not something probabilistic at all. People who think that human free will is a product of the probabilistic nature of subatomic particles do not realize that our 'focus of mind' or conscious understanding and our subjectivity is absolutely dependent on each physically separate quantum energy state. We can change our 'focus of mind' or conscious concentration in different subjects by leaping around on those physically separate quanta (point of consciousness). With this 'focus of mind', we become conscious of any individual subject and this system is very stable for any firm-minded human being. If there was any uncertainty remained with those energy states, we wouldn't be able to concentrate on any subject and, therefore, we couldn't come to logical conclusions to understand anything. When uncertainty cannot ensure consciousness, our conscious choices cannot be the product of any uncertainty anyway. So, what can we say about the experimentally proven uncertainties in the fundamental level? The-I-theory says this is just an apparent feature that has been interpreted incorrectly. We already understood that the universe is created for consciousness, and consciousness gives the existence or reality to anything in the universe. When consciousness concentrates on any system to understand its feature, the specific system gets the reality. We see everything distinct around us because we (conscious agents) live at this level of the universe. At the fundamental level, there is no distinct feature of anything, everything is vague (it doesn't need to be distinct in favor of consciousness), but that doesn't mean everything is uncertain there. When we concentrate on a single feature on the fundamental level, it must get vivid to us because it must show its existence of the moment. This is why there is no distinct velocity and position of particles before we concentrate on it. Another thing is we cannot get both features at the same time because, for consciousness, it is impossible to focus on multiple systems at the same time at any physical levels. At our level, we can ignore the interim gaps when switching to another system, wherein the fundamental level we cannot. We cannot do it even with machines because that are also created by those particles, basically (wave particle duality, uncertainty principle, double slit experiment and quantum entanglement will be explained according to the-I-theory in the expanded version). Here we can assume that there is no uncertainty and randomness remained in the whole physical universal system; apparent uncertainty in the subatomic level is just the product of consciousness only. So how can we have our free will? Unlike compatibilists, we think that freewill and determinism is logically incompatible, but we certainly have our freewill—how is that possible. The-I-theory defines freewill is an essential component of consciousness and all conscious agents have it. First-person—the nonphysical 'bubble of consciousness—not only have the ability to take decisions freely, it also can conduct the agent's body purposefully with its own accord. **Persuaded by the inevitable condition the energy of the universal existence (EUX) acquired this authority to override the deterministic system creating a new kind of system called organisms.** As a result, we can move our limbs to do something incomputable and unpredictable to others. We remember, professor Stephen Hawking asked in his book, *The grand design,* "if we have free will, wherein the evolutionary tree did it develop?" If now we want to answer his question, we must say that organisms are different from inorganic systems only with their consciousness and free will. So, definitely, consciousness and freewill appeared with the first organisms with the starting of evolutionary process. Though, first organisms had been conducted by the UEX mainly with instincts—a prolonged effective collective force—which is an essential component in the evolutionary process. Consciousness and free will in organisms got the maturity in humans, completing the whole process of evolution. This is the postulated mechanism of free will according to the-I-theory, but now the logical part, how can we be sure that we have free will. Despite of all vagueness about free will our rational understanding says, if we do not have our freedom of choices, we won't be able to understand anything. It doesn't need so much insight to understand the fact that no conscious understanding is actually needed when there are no options or choices. If we are always driven by systems and when we have nothing to do about it, why we need to think about anything we are doing right or wrong, and why this should affect our feelings? At this point, intelligent is unnecessary and consciousness is useless in absolute bindings of laws. Here we have still something to understand about humans. Here you can understand one fundamental difference between you and a computer; where you both may have predominant causes created by your respective systems; in your case, you can ignore them whenever you wish, but the computer cannot (I bet you wouldn't like it with your computer if it could). What is something so special about humans that they could ignore the predominant causes by taking authority over the systems in their brain? This is how you can move a stone with your hands in no cause, which is not supposed to be moved without a cause created by the laws of physics. This is how your first-person achieves intelligence or consciousness so that it can understand its own existence and the existence of the rest of the universe. This is exactly what the -I-theory says in the essential properties of first-person consciousness. First-person is freed from the bindings of the laws from the moment it is created. As we have already understood, this system started elementary from the first living organisms and got its perfection in the human level. Here, the first-person rides on you, grab the steering wheel, and drives you away which way it (you) want. When first-person gets eyes with your senses, gets instincts with your instincts, gets consciousness with your consciousness, it can drive you high above sky sometimes; and it can let you down abyss any time. You cannot blame it for its deeds because it is definitely you, and nothing but you.

Let us see how your first-person let you make your choices practically in reality. At first, try to realize some facts about your brain activities. In general, the cerebrum in your brain controls the balance of your body with the help of the inner eye. If this system goes out of order then you could not keep your balance, you could not stay standing on your feet, you will fall down. You think this is what the universal system does; it makes our body able to remain standing on our feet. But, the reality is, if our consciousness fails, you won't be able to remain standing on your feet, even while your balance system is in its full functionality. When a patient with Hysteria gets fainted (loses consciousness), she can fall down instantly from standing; this is because her sensory organs loose connections with the outer environment and her body doesn't find any authority, or any orders to execute about body-balance system. Our point is, your first-person consciousness takes the decision to keep you standing, and it keeps you standing with effort, or authoring on your bodily functions. Your first-person acts as an authority, or a driver of your body.

When you walk on a street, you pass peoples or vehicles avoiding collisions with them. You think your instincts save you from any collision; but, actually, it doesn't. Your instincts can only give you warnings about any upcoming collision by rushing *adrenaline* hormone in your blood stream. What saves you, in these situations, is your conscious decision only, which prompt you with force to move away to avoid any upcoming collision. When you are walking on the road a little out of mind, or being concentrated in another subject not related to your destination, your consciousness (focus of first-person) still switches from that thinking and keep concentrating on the road simultaneously. That is why you do not collide with something when you are walking a bit out of mind. If your first-person fully concentrates on the subject you are thinking and doesn't switch to the road, you will must go to collide. It is not your destiny what saves you when you drive a car, what saves you is your ability to drive, your warning of instincts and, most importantly, your conscious decision—which way you'd move the steering. Without the focus of your first-person you will fail to recognize what you are seeing on the road, you will fail to recognize what you are hearing; even your body wouldn't know what to do when you are thinking something else but doesn't switch to the road frequently and simultaneously. A conscious human cannot remain without concentrating on at least one subject at any moment. There is nothing predominantly acts upon first-person that's supposed to drive a car perfectly on a road in total uncertain (incalculable) situations. The present situation and the courses of upcoming vehicles make deciding first-person what to do in every moment of driving with the help of experience and instincts, and gives the effort in time to save you.

The universal system creates the predominant causes in our brain and stores in our memories as a chemical signature. These predominant causes act as a trigger point (precursors) to make a specific decision. Our regular routine tasks, like going to school or office, are conducted by those predominant causes generally. But we can deny to go to school or office for no reason at all. How can we do this? We can do this, because our first-person can change these trigger points suppressing those predominant causes, and can make us do whatever we want. Yes, it can suppress. Despite of the influence predominant causes, first-person can choose anything from situations and can give priority to anything in making decisions. It can suppress your predominant causes associated with your desire, hunger, thirst, greed, anger, emotions as long as you want. Is also can suppress predominate causes related to your duties, morals, ethics. That is why we can ignore our morals when sometimes we need to meet our necessity, and sometime we can ignore our duties when we need to emphasis on our morality. We humans are mixed with these natural good and bad things. If we were programmed robots, then we were not able to make controls over these things; we would be either very good like angels, or very bad like demons, defined by our genes, but none of us is like that for sure.

Therefore, we can see we have our fate created by the strict laws of the universal system and at the same time, we have 'no fate' as we can change it giving efforts to change the decisions. So our future is destined in one way, and the other way we can change our destiny as we can change our decisions with efforts.

If you are still confused about whether we have free will or not, try to solve a very simple paradox. We can name this "The paradox of knowing". Think about a situation where you must have to make a decision. Suppose you have come to know from a reliable source that you are going to be murdered, (this is quite extreme, but take it for instance) by an assassin, on a specific day in a specific place—suppose, in your home. The source, from whom you have the information, is your best friend whom you trust, or suppose; you could read the mind of the assassin. Our focus will be on the day of the event, or the time when you are going to be murdered. The event is going to be occurring on a day in the future and you have come to know about it previously. Our question is, could you change your destiny at this situation and save you from being murdered? We all know the answer. The answer is yes you can. If you are sure about the day and place of the event then you can save the day for yourself just avoiding that day staying at home. For special security, you can kill that man before he kills you (It seems outrageous, but we think this is much easier than killing the assassin's grandfather traveling back in time so that he couldn't be born). One way or the other, you can save yourself if you want, this is for sure. So if you have previously come to know about the place and time of any future event you can surely avoid that event if you want to avoid it. Now come to the paradoxical part; suppose that the universe is all deterministic and you, somehow, come to know all the systems of the universe from the beginning till end. You can calculate every event with one hundred percent accuracy. Your activities are also within the universal system, so you can calculate your future systems and thus you come to know that you are destined to be murdered on a specific day in a specific place (in your home likely). This situation is identical to your previous situation, only the difference in knowing. Previously you came to know from a reliable source or by reading the assassin's mind and now you have come to know as you are knowing everything—like a God. Again, our question is, could you change your destiny and save yourself from being murdered in this situation? If the universe is all deterministic, If the system of the universe defines our fate, if we don't have free will, if we don't have our choices, if we are programmed robots, we could not change the system and we could not save ourselves from being murdered.

How can this be possible? How can a man who knows something can change his fate but who knows everything can't? Do you have any solution of this apparent paradox? We wish you had.

Another judgment day

Despite of several Crusades, religious savageness, extremism, minority discrimination, inhuman casting system and other religious dysfunctions, some people like to think that a religious environment is necessary for living our life socially. They used to say that religion can give a human being his or her moral stability, mental security; it can keep humans in social bindings, and these bindings, which are stronger than community or even nationality, help our civilization to exist firmly. However, this is true that deformation in religion can affect the nucleus of a strong empire (as like Christianity for Roman Empire), and the most dominant superpowers can easily be declined within a small span of time, but the influence made by religion continues over long, long time upon human beings. Mongol warrior Temujin, Attila the Hun, and Greek warrior Alexander conquered almost half of the world known those days, but their empire destroyed soon after they died. On the contrary, an ill-fated youth from

Bethlehem, a thinker shepherd from the Arab deserts, and a frustrated wanderer from the foot of the Himalayas built their empire to make it last for thousands of years.

It is undeniable that religion always has its strong impact over the human mind and this is also undeniable that these are all man made. An average human being, with a rational mind can easily understand the contradictions between religious belief and the reality around us, but seems like they don't want to understand. We can realize that there is a reason why general people always want to remain under the influence of religion, but why educated intellectuals should believe in these fairy tales. There, maybe, several causes of that and one definitely is skepticism. There are so many confused or self-claimed skeptic remains among intellectuals who don't know how to erase a God from their mind while the universe always gives the sign of a purpose.

A single God plays the prime character role in most of the prominent religious theaters. In religious books, God is defined as the highest supernatural being with its highest supernatural power. In most of the cases, God is idealized as omnipresent, omnipotent, omniscient and, probably, anything you can say with a prefix 'Omni'. Christianity and Muslim religions have such a single God who is independent of the universe and the creator of it. Other religions have different God systems. Polytheism has several different Gods or deities depending on their duties. Ancient Egyptian, Greek, Roman religion and Hinduism, are the most prominent in this class. It seems, a God system is absolutely necessary for making the structure of a religion. There are only exceptions in Buddhism and Confucianism. However, one can easily distinguish Buddhism and Confucianism from other religions, as these (Buddhism and Confucianism) are only ideological teachings of two great philosophers. In Hinduism Gods descends on the human body as incarnations or avatars. Lord Krishna and Rama are considered such incarnations of Gods. In Egyptian, Mesopotamian and Ancient Chinese Polytheism, some of the kings or even the whole dynasty was considered as incarnations of Gods. Pharaohs and the emperors of Qin dynasty can be named as an example. There are several spiritual beliefs where the followers sometimes diverge from the traditional concept of God system. Pantheism is well known among them and where God is considered as a totality of the universe, and this is independent of human transcendence. We have found the names of many prominent scholars, from Marcus Aurelius to Frederic Hegel and from Giordano Bruno to Albert Einstein, associated with pantheism. Thinkers of Pandeism, Monist idealist pantheism, and Duelist pantheism are, whatsoever, admirers of human consciousness or cosmic consciousness from a spiritual point of view. We would like to distinguish the-I-theory from these concepts in the expanded edition of this book. Here our purpose is only to emphasis on the concept of a single omnipresent, omnipotent and omniscient God who is the creator of the universe, and who is independent of the universal system. We want to do this to overrule the concepts of the so-called intelligent designers who try to prove the universe as the result of a "divine design" only to establish this kind of concept of a God. You can think, this concept of a purposeful universe created by an independent God has its ninety percent evidence of eligibility; but one percent infeasibility is enough for declination of any concept or theory when the infeasibility is at the base of that concept. In this compact chapter, we shall see that the concept of a unique, almighty God, independent of the universe that apparently creates the primary ground the 'intelligent design' theory, would be the main factor for the declination of the same theory.

Let us make our views more clear. Intelligent design is supported by a supernatural entity, with all the characteristics of a unique almighty God, like as seen in the Christian and Muslim religions. Intelligent design is at least a theory of the universe, so we cannot just let it supported on the head of Don Quixote. This theory needs such a thing to support it, which has all the qualities of a God and there must not remain any gap or any kind of incapability in its qualities. There may be a thousand ways to find a hole in traditional God theories (Richard Dawkins and Christopher Hitchens may have their lists). We can leave alone those 'serious' questions like, "Can God heal the amputees?", or, "Why God seems disfavors the vulnerable?" and some others like that, but we can certainly expect that God must have the ability of experiencing literally anything that it creates, and there cannot be anything existed that it (God) is unable to experience. This should be the most decisive quality for a candidate of an omnipresent, omnipotent and omniscient God, which would supposedly support intelligent design as the ultimate theory of the universe.

Fortunately or unfortunately, the I-theory can justify the eligibility of any kind of candidate for a God who wants to be crowned as the creator. We have been told from some of the religions that God has a Judgment day for each and every one of us, but now we dare to say that we have another judgment day for God as well. There may have thousands of books to prove the existence of God, but we have only one question to justify his candidacy as a God.

Our question is very simple and straightforward, "Can God experience the first-person (subjective consciousness) of a human being?" The answer must be 'yes' as the God should be able to experience anything it creates. But there is a little problem with that affirmative thinking that can crash our belief and banish us immediately in hell!

Suppose you are standing before the God. You have your first-person and the God has his first-person (whomever he may be, if he is an entity, he must have first-person). So, You are a third-person to God, and God is a third-person to you. You cannot experience the self-consciousness of God (as this is impossible). But God should have the ability to experience your self-consciousness as he created you, and logically he cannot create anything without experiencing it. So, let us assume, God can experience your first-person. This is the way it should be, shouldn't it? But here the problem comes: when the God is experiencing your first-person, he is getting the self-experience as you are getting now—not more than that, not less than that. Literally, he must have to replace with you, and must remain confined in you to get your first-person. Therefore, In this situation, God is nothing more than you. Do you think this is possible? On the other hand, when God replaces in you, you are also getting his self-consciousness through first-person. So you are then literally nothing but the God, is this also possible? Can a God be just nothing but a human? And can a human being be the omnipotent, omniscient, omnipresent God for any moment? If we think that God can make a human experiencing God's own first-person, then the human, at the very moment, is nothing but God and the God is nothing but a human. This is a situation of taking over each-other's self-experience physically and practically. However, this situation is supposed to be possible. But If the situation is possible then it is contradictory with both human and God—as this is impossible that you can be a God for any moment. If this situation is impossible then this is also contradictory with God's quality that he has a fundamental incapability of experiencing your first-person.

This situation is not a paradox. It clearly indicates that first-person is a subjective platform and it cannot be lower or higher. It is same for everyone including God. You feel your first-person such a way and if there is a God exists then he also might feel his first-person the same way. If God makes any influence over your first-person with his supernatural power, he won't be able to experience you precisely. So, anyone wants to feel the first-person of yours, he or she must remain confined in your body, and has to feel it the same way you feel; there is no shortcut way of that for anybody, even if the candidate is as mighty as a God.

This apparent paradox clearly indicates that there is one thing exists between God and you, as all first-persons are the same. Almighty God and you, both can't exist holding the same kind of first-persons. Now you decide yourself, which one you would consider exists between you or the God—the choice is yours.

Evidence in the Evolution

The theory of Biological Evolution about the origin of species on earth is one of the most valuable theories in the history of science. Since Charles Darwin, the prime proponent of this theory, there have been numerous researches conducted in support or in opposition of this theory, and now it is well established as an empirical fact rather than a conceptual theory. The descriptive area is very diverse and wide on this subject. This would be nothing but an audacity if we try to explore the entire evolutionary process in just one— short chapter; therefore, we shall only go through a brief, comparative discussion here on the traditional concept of evolution with the startling findings of the-I-theory. I-theory remains incomplete without explaining the key factors of evolution, because these explanations directly provide considerable practical evidence in support of this theory.

The word "evolution" means slow change. The theory of evolution is about a slow-changing process of the living things, occurs across successive generations to create well-adaptable traits by random mutation and repeated speciation. According to Darwinism, evolution is regulated by means of natural selection—a process of removing harmful mutations, and spreading beneficial mutations all over the generations. Darwinism also refers evolution as a nonrandom but unguided process. Subjective universal model (described in the expanded edition of this book) of the-I-theory does not refute the existing mechanism of evolution theory, rather it tries to reestablish evolution on a concrete base proposing a significant modification of the concept of natural selection in a subjective manner, what we shall call, **Targeted conscious selection in favor of supreme consciousness (human consciousness)**. The main concept is, biological evolution is regulated by the Energy of the universal existence as a collective 'nonphysical' force persuaded by the inevitable condition. The Energy of universal existence initiates evolution in the first organisms directly overriding on deterministic systems with the help of free will, only to create and sustain one species favorable for supreme consciousness. The-I-theory proposes this "Targeted conscious selection" as the mechanism that resolves all misconceptions about the biological evolution process and fills all so-called 'gaps' in its consistency. Moreover, implementation of the-I-theory answers all fundamental questions regarding biological development that Darwinism does not intend to answer, and as a result, it comes to an outstanding conclusion resolving the egoistic problem of humans to accept primates as their ancestors.

Subjective universal model of The-I-theory solves three fundamental problems of evolution, these are:

1. Why there is only one intelligent species created in the whole evolutionary process amongst millions of species. (The word "intelligent" may seem controversial to many people. Some may consider Cetacean animals like, whales, dolphins are intelligent and self-conscious of some extent. This is true, but we humans can legitimately ignore the argument as long as any cetacean animal does not come with it.)

2. How the first transition happened from the non-living level of the first self-replicating cells (Abiogenesis). This is the famous Chicken-egg problem which actually "engine first or body first" according to biological evolution.

3. Why there a biological evolutionary process exists at all? This is one of the most fundamental and important question of all. Darwinism or Neo-Darwinism does not answer this why question, why was the universe in need such a process to create living things completely different from the previous systems of the universe.

As we have stated earlier, the key concept of evolution according to the-I-theory is that, the energy of the universal existence (EUX) 'solely' governs the whole process of evolution. Biological evolution was not initiated purposelessly without any target; instead, it is a long-persisting process of the energy of universal existence, which continues obstinately on a course of action in spite of difficulties, opposition and frequent failure. This is the action of the same nonphysical energy that inevitably, but unconsciously, created the physical universe. The conscious process of evolution is not any preexisting consciousness of the universal energy itself, rather it is a collective consciousness acquired through all living things from their correlations to the universal system. Evolution occurs at species level and it concentrates on the survival of every species created; but who cares, and why cares, about the survival or extinction of any species? What is the contribution of living organisms within this deterministic universal system? The-I- theory proposes that the Energy of Universal Existence, which is only a fruit of the inevitable condition that acted predominantly, had been searching continuously for the Eye (supreme consciousness) by creating a variety of primordial living organisms and had continued developing them as long as it had reached its goal. This was like a scientific method to achieve a specific result. EUX has no way to understand previously which organism is eligible for supreme consciousness. So it persistently experimented with living organisms, creating a variety of traits and maintaining their survival or extinction in a process that we call evolution. EUX not only regulated random mutation, it also compared the result and accepted or rejected any trait, which ultimately led to speciation or extinction of any existing species. EUX encoded the information in the genes and passed through successors, because this was the only way of doing it—as EUX is nonphysical—it has no brain or memories. In this sense, evolution is not a previously designed process to create humans; evolution is just the long-persistent action of the EUX, targeted to create something unknown that meets the criteria of a true recognizing agent of universal existence. Intelligent designers, and who sees design in evolution and in genes must come to realize the fact that the purpose of any design should be reducing the time and wrong choices to get a nearly perfect outcome. But evolution is a process which is sometimes huge time elapsing and sometimes hasty, and with abundance of wrong outcomes. This is, actually, a successful (this is what it meant to be) experiment initiated with a preexisting target but regulated with no design. We have learnt previously that first-person was freed (free will) from the first-living organisms and thus all primordial organisms can have a certain level of consciousness, but these did not fulfill the criteria of existence with a proper consciousness of first-person. Therefore, the energy of the universal existence (inevitable condition) searched for its goal persistently; at last, it fulfilled the condition of supreme consciousness in human beings, and then sustained the position by bridling evolution. Therefore, according to I-theory evolution can be termed as a **targeted conscious process of biological development,**

regulated collectively by the energy of the universal existence, by means of cancelling unnecessary traits and applying emphasis on importance in favor of supreme consciousness.

The elaborated evolutionary process is as follows according to the-I-theory:

1. The process of biological development regulated and conducted collectively by the Energy of universal existence (inevitable condition) to meet the target of creating one species eligible for supreme consciousness.
2. Variety of species originated from the distinct variation of primordial organisms (not from a single universal common ancestor).
3. EUX consciously approves or cancels any species, which are, respectively, promising or futile for supreme consciousness.
4. Major and rapid speciation only occur after a huge geological or environmental change, creating directly full-sized new set of organisms, completely different from their ancestors, adaptable to new environment.

So, we get some distinct differences in the evolution process with Darwinism and the-I-theory. First of all, In Darwinism or Neo-Darwinism, evolution process is not directed to a target. Speciation occurs only to create adaptable species, which fits for survival in a changeable environment. I-theory proposes targeted conscious evolution to create humans for a certain period of stable environment. According to the-I-theory, the whole universal system is created and regulated targeted to supreme consciousness. Biological evolution is the secondary and final part of the complete universal development. All evolutionists know that natural selection does not occur randomly. It becomes neater with modification. This gives obvious sign of a collective force, which consciously try to modify the system with a target. In Absence of any guiding force, evolution process would have gone Topsy-turvy and uncertain. This force also maintains ecological functions by developing relationships between organisms and inorganic environment. If there was no supporting force behind, several components of ecosystems including energy flow, predator-prey cycles, instincts and food chain could not have been preserved for a long period of time. We have clear evidence of this nonphysical energy that acts collectively with all living organisms everywhere in the evolutionary process. Instincts remain encoded in the genes of individual organisms that is acquired through experiences and passed to offspring. Instincts of the living organism act beyond their physical senses and it is pointed to the survival of every individual organism of a population. Which care about and why for the survival of a living organism beyond their senses? What difference it would make to the universe if all the living things on this planet go to extinction? Obviously, instincts and all other features of evolution are initiated and held together manually (consciously) by an energy which concerns about extinction of any individual organism or any species. How plants come to know they have to bloom for insets, how trees know their seeds can be spread-out far away through water and air, how some sea turtles and ells know they have to go to Saragossa, how Grunions know there is a second wave waiting for them, how Salmons go back their spawning ground—these are some ordinary evidences of survival maneuvers of organisms that EUX operates collectively beyond the physical senses(sight, hearing, touch etc.) of living things.

Secondly, In Darwinism or Neo-Darwinism, evolution is only hereditary, and information is only preserved by individual genes in all living things; so in the case of mass extinction (extinction of all living things including or excluding the primordial living organisms) further evolution process will conduct in the same rate with the former process. But according to the-I-theory, the information is preserved by the energy of universal existence collectively through the genes of all living things, and in the case of mass extinction next evolution process can be speeded up by directly cancelling unnecessary species of the former evolution. There can be 'abrupt leap' happened in speciation, within the regular course of natural selection, when EUX gets some promising traits within a single organism of any given population. The mystery of the Cambrian explosion (explosive creation of invertebrate with complex eyes after Cambrian mass extinction) can be resolved this way.

Thirdly, In the process of evolution called

Darwinism, natural selection always maintains survival of the fittest species, and it is an everlasting continuous process for all organisms. However, in the-I-theory, evolution process regulates consciously to reach a target, which is to create a single species eligible for supreme consciousness, and this process (searching a special species with required traits of supreme consciousness) stops immediately after reaching this target. On the other hand, when it has this prime target, evolution process does not actually concentrate on any other species that are only eligible for survival but does not show any pre-qualities of achieving supreme consciousness. Here is the main point of this modification. Evolution functionally stopped for humans after supreme consciousness took over. There is no remarkable speciation is going to happen to humans in near or far future. Even in major geographical and environmental changes, other species can experience further evolution or can go extinct, but we are not going to split into Eloi and Morlocks.

Finally, we know there are several problems with Darwinian evolution. One of the main problem is the absence of intermediate transitional living organisms (not only transitional fossils). When natural selection occurs continuously, and, relatively, with the same rate of every species, then we are certainly going to see more transitional intermediates than new species at any given time within the existing species. With refers from Darwinism, we can expect to see some primates are coming down from the trees and trying to stand on two feet giving signature of our ancestors. One common excuse for this inconsistency in Darwinism is that natural selection took place for over millions of years in on a given population to create new species. However, this proposition can become boomerang, because the more time takes for speciation, the more intermediate species we would expect to see at any certain period of time.

There are other problems of evolution like those controversies about developing organisms with complex eyes in a normal evolutionary process, and about current evidence of speciation only in lower level organisms. Targeted conscious selection process of the-I-theory easily resolves these apparent gaps in evolution. When EUX is conscious in some broader extent (collectively with all organisms), have free will, and have a target, it can do more than Darwinism can expect. The-I-theory suggests that major speciation occurred at every level of organisms after a mass extinction (after a huge geological and environmental change). These new set of species was fully different from their predecessors in size, traits and diversity, and adaptable to new environments. Therefore, humans (Homo sapiens) came from the new set of species after the extinction of the dinosaurs. Humanoids like Homo habilis, Homo erectus and Neanderthals are other species of the same genus, which appeared with the same incident. Apes and monkeys are always in another genus, also living around the same period. Humanoids had been always bipeds, omnivorous, and could do little tasks using their brain. Perhaps the Homo sapiens were sensitive and vulnerable among humanoids, and they may have fewer hairs in their body like us, so they started cave life protecting cold and other threats. According to the-I-theory, other humanoids of the genus did not extinct losing the race of survival in the wild due to their underdeveloped brain than humans; they had been eliminated intentionally by the EUX, protecting only one species for supreme consciousness. This question is not worth asking why the energy of the universal existence maintained just one species for supreme consciousness—we can clearly imagine if intelligent extraterrestrial beings (aliens) try to share the same planet with humans what is going to happen.

About the other problems of evolution, the-I-theory suggests that EUX can concentrate on a specific organ depending on its necessity (on stipulation "emphasize on importance"). So Cambrian complex-eyed species was not unusual by any means.

Now about those fundamental questions that evolution does not commit to answer; we are going to start with the chicken-egg problem. This problem refers to abiogenesis, which assumes that simple organic molecules spontaneously developed into complex nucleoids and these nucleoid chain creates RNA molecules; Subsequently, the RNA molecule 'somehow' learned self-replicating, and after that, natural selection occurred. Anyone can ask, if RNA molecules could spontaneously develop, then why they need another process of production? Self-replication ability of RNA indicates that developing from non-living to RNA molecules was not easy and was not spontaneous; a force, surely, had backed it up, and this force held on this unstable system until the natural selection process took over. Since after EUX took control on self-replication by natural selection the first transit system from non-living to living organisms collapsed; and we are never going to see them again. This is unusual but the fact is, EUX created a living engine directly which had the ability to create its body, and had the ability to reproduce (explained in the expanded version). In this regard, we can conclude that a mature chicken already conceived with eggs first came out of nowhere; or chicken and egg came at the same time.

Now it is easy to understand why there is an evolutionary process exists, or why living things exist at all, and why the universe wasn't just happy with its inorganic assets. Supreme consciousness gives EUX the true feeling of existence. Without experiencing from supreme consciousness, EUX could never understand about its own existence or the existence of the universe. Understanding was impossible within a law-binding, deterministic universe. That is why EUX started a complete different system (living organisms) to get a certain level of independence even remaining within the bindings of the laws. This living system led to supreme consciousness (human consciousness level), because this is the level where intelligence can arise. So when EUX gets the perfect feeling of existence it can justify it with the help of intelligence. That is why we ask, "Who am I?", "Where have I come from?", or "How am I existed?"

Conclusion: The reasoning

Can the universe create itself? If we think, before the creation of the universe there was no previous phase of it then, scientifically or unscientifically, it is not absurd at all to think that one thing that is not existed at all cannot organize, or merely, cannot give guidance to create itself.

Can the universe come out from quantum fluctuations without any reason? Many scientists feel happy with this explanation because they normally observe that some quantum objects are always coming out spontaneously in the subatomic level without any definite reasons. However, the universe is not just filled with fluctuated quantum objects. There are also definite physical laws, which strictly guide those quantum objects and tell them what to do in the first place; and those laws never change in their characteristics—that is why we see a universe like this. Which gives those laws such inflexible character that keep them unchanged forever to give stability of the universe? Why gravity (curvature of space-time?) just doesn't refuse to bind objects at any situation? Why electrons never refuse to decay in neutrons without a very extreme situation?

Can Jesus's –Moses's- Abraham's God create the universe? If we sacrifice our all rationale and try to establish God as the creator of the universe, then humans are certainly out of the universe, because, the way God creates something, it is not possible to create a single 'human with first-person' the same way.

So how the universe was created? We have many evidences which tell us that the universe must have at least one starting point (with a big bang or something else). So, why, how and where it started to come to the condition as it is now? Nobody can deny that we have been living our lives happily without having a rational answer on this with any satisfying theory from the beginning of civilization till now. Most of us did not find this much annoying because we always thought that we have just one life to pass, and after that, there have been only two options remaining for two popular groups of 'believers'—eternity or nothing. Unexpectedly, the-I-theory brings us headache back with those thoughts, as it seems it (the-I-theory) doesn't support neither of those two options.

By analyzing all of our preceding discussions, we supposed to understand that there is a quite different flow of reality going on behind our normal life-and-death scenario. There is also a different destination waiting for the whole universe. Probably the universe is not indestructible, but we know from the-I-theory that nonexistence as a whole is impossible—as it is undetectable and indefinable. So which is indestructible is only existence as a whole. Now, the question is what could be the definition of existence as a whole? The answer is now obvious—our first-person that gives the subjective experience is the definition of true existence, nothing more or less. Here the inevitable condition arises even before the universe created. This inevitable condition acted as potential energy and induced a nonphysical active energy (EUX) like a force, to come into existence creating the whole universe unconsciously (only rejecting the inappropriate no matter how long it takes), and creating humans consciously (evolving persistently with living organisms within a period of stable cosmic environment). Multiple living first-persons at the same time is the most complicated mechanism ever developed by this force. EUX not only creates true existence, it also sustains its position strongly with free will and consciousness. What we do with our free will is the will of this energy. This free will of the EUX with the help of encoded instincts (survival maneuvers acquired collectively through experience and inherited through genes) makes humans and other organisms survive longer in this hostile world. We have understood that first-person subjective consciousness cannot arise from any local system either spontaneously or by a spell. It came out as an ontological property with a very complex and time elapsing system of the energy of universal existence.

But this is obvious that no system can be predesigned, in an intelligent way, by this energy as it is incapable of having any foresight and thus unable to predict anything. It can only try all the way rejecting the futile protecting the promising ones; it actually did the same thing here before humans.

Most of us also hold a spurious believe that the whole universal system is mathematical. We use to think that everything can be explained in terms of mathematics, but this is not true at all. We do not realize that there is something always remains beyond mathematics—is an existence. Except some philosophers, even mathematicians do not know that all mathematics comes after existence. The digit one (1) is not belongs to any mathematics; it is the fundamental existence. We cannot explain the one (1) with any mathematics or with any of its formulas. When this fundamental existence (one) starts replicating itself, or splits into two, mathematics starts. What we can do with this fundamental one (1) if it is not allowed to divide into multiples? If, somehow, the physical universe destroys, the inevitable condition or true existence remains as one (1). It is indestructible. There is nothing like zero (0) in this universal system which is absolute nonexistence (nonexistence gaps within the transmission of particles is not a part of universal system). So 1 (one) can never go to zero. If the universe destroys, the energy of universal existence will induce again right away creating another universe same like this. This is the perpetual cycle of universal existence. If it never destroys, it will always remain as existence—just keep changing shape.

Some are fascinated by the laws of physics, but now we know, these are just laws in favor of true existence, the first-person subjective consciousness. First-person needs those to create a steady logical base, that is why they are not allowed to change their characteristics. Professor Stephen Hawking asked three fundamental questions about the laws in his book The Grand Design, *"What is the origin of the laws?", "Are there any exceptions to the laws, i.e., miracles?", "Is there only one set of possible laws?".* Traditional physics cannot answer these questions, but we are now convinced that we can answer these easily in terms of the-I-theory. Inevitable condition of self-recognition of the universal existence is the origin of all laws and systems. Universal system does not allow any exception of the laws, or miracles, that's supposed to disrupt consciousness from its logical base (though the system is not full-proof, there have unexpected incidences caused by the same system). And there is just one set of laws possible that confirms consciousness.

According to the-I-theory, The energy of universal existence conducted evolution targeted to create a special species, humans, which is capable of having supreme consciousness (first-person subjective consciousness). It searched for this species experimenting with different organisms in different environments for a long period of time. At last, it not only created this 'promised' species, also ensured its survival directly taking over it. Evolution stopped in its further development of the superior species after creating modern humans. Now the EUX sustains the survival of this creature with a new system called intelligence. Intelligence is much easier and quicker process of survival than evolution. Applying this new process, at first it invented the use of fire, then harvesting, farming; later Penicillin, Electricity, computers and iPhones. Now the EUX is self-conscious and self-confined, that is why sometimes it asks about its own origin, and sometime about the origin of the universe. This energy is nonphysical (not sensible or detectable physically like thermal energy) and it creates and holds the whole universe. However, we cannot replace this energy of the universal existence with our traditional God concept anyway, because this energy was not intelligent at all before it develops into humans. It was not even smart like a three-year-old human child before Pleistocene Epoch. It didn't know the simple equation "two and two makes four" before a human discovered it. It has no separate brain, no memory, and no storage system of information except by living creatures. So, how can we honor it as God? The EUX obtains all properties and characteristics of matters, energies and forces. This ability may seem amazing but these are just obtained automatically persuaded by the inevitable condition. The EUX also correlates with the matter and energies to get a collective sense of everything. It catches the sense of individuality by separating first-persons physically at the fundamental level. But, As a matter of fact, through the whole universal development and biological evolutionary process EUX only compared which was in favor of first-person and which was not. It had never seen a glimpse of true intelligence before a human mind. Even after it 'possesses' into humans, its intellectual development is not at all satisfactory compared to God. It surely does not understand Gravity much better than Albert Einstein; and, probably, it does not understand Investment better than Warren Buffett. So consideration of this energy as God will certainly be contradictory with the grandeur of our traditional omniscient God.

The-I-theory reveals the 'secret' mechanism of emerging the universe and our first-person consciousness. The theory unveils the reality from behind the black curtain of universal theater. It explains the way how we born as an individual person and live our life with others. The-I-theory says that we all feel the same pain, and all other subjective feelings, from just separate points of consciousness. It says, subjectively, we have no death—there is no destruction of our 'self,' we are living immortals, and we are going to live here along the eternity. This is our preordained fate to be born as a human being, and to die to be another. There is no escape for anyone us from this infinite cycle. Individual persons are nothing but their memory. When a human dies, her memory destroys with her body, but she still remains alive with other living human bodies. We cannot say that she is going to 'have' any specific living person after her death, because her personality is not going to transfer to any specific person. The system is, the EUX will just lose one confinement of first-person subjectivity after her death among billions, and she will remain as one of the living humans—just as she is one of the living humans now. There is no physical or mathematical system involved here that you can trace your next life. Although this is true that he or she is also going to be a newborn baby maintained by the very next point of consciousness. This next point of consciousness can be in any kind of organisms. However, other organisms, including animals, do not feel confinement; probably, due to their inconsistent long-term memory and thinking incapability (we humans also do not feel individual confinement all the time, especially, when we do something with mass enthusiasm). So you are not going to be a bat after you die this is for sure. The next point of consciousness can be created anywhere in the world, or in any other planet in the universe where supreme consciousness likely to exist. Sarcastically, this may be the only way of fulfilling our dreams of intergalactic travel—fueled by our death! However, your next life in another galaxy will not express much difference with your previous 'earthly' life. A planet with approximately the same size and mass, slightly tilted in axis, relatively the same distance from the sun, filled with much water than land and maybe not more than one moon; and you are going to be born as a normal human being as you are now. So life is going to be sweeter and hazardous there, as same like here now. This can be a matter of real argument whether extraterrestrial intelligent life really exists or not. We see EUX maintains the survival of humans by giving a complex life-death cycle for a limited time. It cannot give human's life at a stretch forever, because the hospitable environment of this planet has a definite lifespan related to the lifespan of the sun. So why shouldn't we worry about the EUX's plan with us after the sun goes retirement being a Red Giant? There are many things to consider. If the EUX has concentrated to humans only on this planet, there are no other intelligent species (humans) remains in any other planet in the whole universe; because , if the supreme consciousness of any planet cannot ever communicate with supreme consciousness of other planets then it is useless for EUX to hold supreme consciousness on multiple planets. On the other hand, if the earth is destroyed in a cataclysmic event or with the sun burnout, and no other Exoplanets in the universe hold life, EUX will, certainly, lose its 'eye'. So, inevitably it must try to recover the situation as early as it can. We can guess, there may be better systems remain for EUX than waiting till the destruction of the universe and then repeating the whole process. The universe is unimaginably vast. This is not unusual to remain some identical earths, in the Goldilocks zones, of approximately the same age somewhere in this vastness. If this is true, then extraterrestrial civilization exists with exact human-like creatures (not ugly green 'Megaminds'), or at least evolution is going on with other living organisms there. Those possible identical earths can be of the same age, older or younger than the earth, we would expect to see different situations there—some civilizations are highly developed than us, and some are just 'Jurassic park'.

The inevitable theory is a theory of the origin of the universe. It explains the universe successfully by means of first-person subjective consciousness. However, we must realize that this is only a theory. This is not reality. Reality is what we directly feel with our senses. If we write down this theory on the blackboard, or pronounce it verbally, it does not give birth of a universe. Things for a physical theory are the same. The system we could observe and measure physically, we can make a physical theory of those with our thoughts and words, but it is also not reality anyway. We, humans, are the direct absorbers of reality, and we cannot change this reality of direct experience no matter we die or the universe destroys itself. So, there is nothing to worry about what happens to the background universe against our survival; we shall always see us living exactly like this and asking questions like—where have we come from. There is something what we must worry about that we can never die. We shall live here forever with just a life-and death-cycle. This is the cycle of our immortality—each and every one of us is just the part of one, and the one is immortal.

However, the complexity held by the universal system, creating tiny humans to give their life is unthinkable, but this achievement of EUX was not *tour de force*. One can ask, did the EUX learn from mistakes and started over multiple times creating the universe— especially for giving its stability by choosing accurate parameters of gravity and other forces? This question is awfully absurd. All energies and matters are just different forms of EUX itself, and it is totally impossible for EUX to understand anything separately of the universe before it comes to supreme consciousness. From the beginning of the universe to supreme consciousness, it is one uncut process of the EUX by just changing into different shapes in the timelessness. So if we think it upside down that won't make any difference in the process. The question of before-after, past-future is meaningful to us because we have the sense of time. But from the perspective of EUX, questions like, which was created first—consciousness or the universe, has no meaning at all, because it just remains in the same position always in various forms of existence. The EUX had the inevitable condition, so it must knew the way of fulfilling the condition. This is how it could look back to supreme consciousness, standing behind the goal line, before creating the universe. It just bridged upon these two situations (inevitable condition and supreme consciousness) achieving all accurate parameters directly from hundred-percent certainty. Unofficially, this is the 'certainty principle' on which the-I-theory is standing. Certainty in the origin is the reason why we see the universe is fine-tuned; and methodically, it has not been obtained by choosing all accurate forms of parameters. The EUX created and supported the necessary system persuaded by the inevitable condition, and now the inevitable condition is replaced by true existence, so the EUX is now only supporting this existence robustly. We always feel the influence of an unknown united energy in everywhere and in everything acting beyond our senses. For this reason, the sense of Pantheism developed among intellectuals of all times, and lay-people always have the intuition of an omnipresent God. In this sense, the-I-theory does not prove any traditional atheism. This is a theory of another God which remains slumbered into every matter, every energy and in every living thing, and it wakes up divided into the minds of more than seven billion humans. This God is not unworthy of devotion at all. It also established a religion silently all over the world—a religion so powerful and primitive, which is preached by Humanity.

Unveiling the mind of God with the-I-theory

Printed in Great Britain
by Amazon.co.uk, Ltd.,
Marston Gate.